Managing SEO

Leading SEO Programs in an AI-Driven Search World

Ash Nallawalla

Twitter/X: @ashnallawalla

Keywords: C-Suite, Executive Leadership, Digital Strategy, Search Visibility, Organic Search, Corporate Governance, Digital Transformation, AI Search, Large Language Models, SEO Strategy, Digital Risk Management, Marketing ROI

658.4092 : Technology and Application of Knowledge > Management and Auxiliary Services > Management > Executive Leadership and Governance

BUS075000 BUSINESS & ECONOMICS / Leadership

BUS104000 BUSINESS & ECONOMICS / Corporate Governance

BUS043000 BUSINESS & ECONOMICS / Marketing / General

BUS090050 BUSINESS & ECONOMICS / E-Commerce / Search Engine Optimization

TABLE OF CONTENTS

PREFACE

Visibility determines opportunity in a digital economy, yet many leaders are asked to make search engine optimization (SEO) decisions without a clear managerial understanding of how visibility actually works. SEO is often presented as a technical craft, a marketing tactic, or a set of operational tricks. None of those contexts help you to decide how to allocate resources, assess risk, guide teams, or evaluate long-term impact.

This book is written for managers and business owners who need to understand how SEO operates today—across search engines, AI-driven assistants, zero-click environments, and complex digital ecosystems—without becoming specialists or reading multiple prerequisite texts. It is designed for people who are accountable for outcomes, not implementations.

You may not have the time or need to work through the strategic depth of *Accidental SEO Manager*, the governance models in *AI and Web Governance*, the measurement frameworks in *Is Our SEO Working?*, or the organizational analysis in *The C-Suite Blind Spot*. This volume distills the essential ideas that underpin those books and translates them into a coherent, decision-ready model. Nothing here is reused or duplicated from those titles; if you read Books 2 through 5, you will encounter entirely new material. This book equips you quickly. It does not replace the others.

Managers frequently inherit SEO responsibility without training, documentation, or consistent internal processes. They are expected to make decisions about content, platforms, vendors, budgets, and priorities while navigating a search environment that evolves faster than most organizations can absorb. This book gives you a working understanding of SEO as a **business capability**—not a technical specialty and not a marketing silo.

You will learn how modern search systems interpret content, how structure and clarity shape visibility, how AI-generated answers influence decision-making, and how organizations can build systems that keep visibility stable through redesigns, migrations, staff turnover, and shifting priorities. The focus is on **what matters, why it matters, and how to manage it over time**.

The book's structure mirrors how managers approach complex problems. You begin by understanding the environment. You then establish the fundamentals that govern interpretation and visibility. Finally, you apply those principles through systems, workflows, measurement, and organizational design. Early chapters explain how search evolved from keyword matching into semantic interpretation, entity recognition, and AI-driven synthesis. These chapters provide the mental model required to reason about visibility as it exists now, not as it existed a decade ago.

Later chapters translate those principles into operational guidance. You will learn how to evaluate performance without getting lost in tooling, how to strengthen content systems, how to manage visibility across portfolios rather than single sites, and how to design workflows that reduce risk rather than react to it. You will see how reporting, quality assurance, and governance enable informed decisions without requiring technical depth.

Throughout the book, guidance is framed for conversations with stakeholders who may not understand the mechanics of search. SEO is positioned as a durable organizational capability rather than a series of fixes. Visibility trends are treated not as mysterious volatility, but as signals of internal structure, consistency, and clarity. Wherever possible, the emphasis is on prevention, because avoiding instability is far less costly than recovering from it.

By the end of this book, you should be able to lead SEO with confidence. You will know how to support teams without micromanaging, assess vendors and proposals critically, prioritize work rationally, and recognize risks before they escalate. You will also understand how your decisions affect visibility in AI-driven environments where clarity, structure, and conceptual stability matter more than ever.

If you choose to go deeper, the other volumes in this series extend the foundation established here. They are not prerequisites. They are continuations.

This book is a guide to leading visibility in a world where search is no longer a list of 10 blue links, but a network of systems interpreting your organization at scale. Lead with clarity, and the rest becomes manageable.

Melbourne, January 2026

TERMINOLOGY AND CONVENTIONS

Throughout this book, we distinguish between three system types that shape visibility:

- **Search systems** (for example, Google and Bing) index and rank content algorithmically.

- **Large Language Models (LLMs)** (such as ChatGPT, Claude, and Gemini) generate answers and may cite or summarize your content.

- **AI systems** is an inclusive term covering the broader ecosystem, including AI-enhanced search features, assistants, and recommendation platforms.

When the distinction matters, it is stated explicitly. When the principle applies across the ecosystem, the broader term is used.

We use **evaluators** to describe the people using these systems, emphasizing interpretation rather than interaction.
We use **entities** to describe distinct, stable concepts that systems recognize—people, organizations, products, places, or ideas.

The term **pattern** appears throughout the book. In this context, a pattern is a **repeatable, observable structure or behavior that systems rely on to interpret meaning or scale decisions**. Depending on context, this may refer to how pages are structured, how evaluators behave, how AI systems infer intent, or how organizations make consistent choices.

The specific **meaning** (an important concept in this book) is determined by context, but the principle is constant: **visibility at scale depends on stability in repeatable systems**.

Later chapters distinguish between structural, behavioral, interpretive, and operational patterns. The distinctions evolve, but the underlying idea remains the same.

Paragraphs containing important concepts are marked with a border marker such as this one. If you are skimming this book, you should look at those sections first.

Chapter 1

SEO IN A VISIBILITY-DRIVEN ECONOMY

Decisions about structure, ownership, accuracy, and coordination now shape **visibility** more than individual optimizations ever did. In this book, *evaluators* refers to real people using search engines, AI assistants, and discovery platforms to make decisions—not quality raters or internal reviewers.

VISIBILITY AS AN ECONOMIC FORCE

Modern organizations operate in an environment where visibility determines opportunity. Customers discover brands, evaluate products, compare services, and make decisions through digital interfaces long before speaking to a salesperson or entering a store. Search engines, panels, recommendation systems, AI summaries, and conversational assistants now mediate the majority of informational and commercial pathways—each serving as a surface for interpreting and presenting meaning.

Visibility materializes on **surfaces**—the interfaces where search systems and AI systems present, summarize, or reference your organization—and managers influence visibility by ensuring those surfaces can interpret meaning consistently.

In this environment, SEO is neither a marketing tactic nor a technical specialty. It shapes whether your organization is understood, trusted, and accurately represented at the moments that matter—across the surfaces where search systems and AI systems present, summarize, or reference your information. Visibility influences who is considered, which options are compared, and which explanations are accepted as credible.

Visibility functions as a dependency for many other business activities because it determines how reliably those surfaces can interpret and convey meaning. When it is strong, downstream systems interpret your organization consistently. When it is weak, those systems introduce friction, distortion, or omission regardless of product quality or internal effort. Recognition fails when the structure breaks down, meaning drifts, or coordination weakens.

VISIBILITY DRIVES OUTCOMES

Visibility determines whether your information influences decisions across customers, partners, journalists, researchers, and stakeholders. Journeys now begin through typed queries, voice interactions, AI-assisted responses, and emerging discovery interfaces. In all cases, visibility governs whether your organization enters the decision set at all.

High-quality visibility extends influence beyond direct audiences. It shapes how industries understand your positioning, how competitors frame comparisons, and how partners assess credibility. This influence compounds over time as systems reuse, summarize, and reference what they already trust.

Later chapters examine how this shift affects metrics, expectations, and executive communication. At this stage, the key point is simple: **visibility is interpretability at scale.**

YOUR ROLE IN MODERN SEO

SEO is inherently cross-functional. It touches product, engineering, content, design, analytics, legal, and executive decision-making. No single specialist can manage it in isolation. Your role is to shape the conditions that allow visibility to function coherently across teams.

When you understand how visibility works, you diagnose issues more accurately and prioritize with greater confidence. You bring the right teams together at the right moments and frame requirements in language that resonates across disciplines. You position SEO as an operational necessity rather than a discretionary initiative.

In practice, this includes clarifying **ownership** for key surfaces, maintaining the stability of technical systems, ensuring content meets clarity standards, and advocating for infrastructure and template decisions that protect meaning over time. You also shape executive understanding. Leaders rely on you to explain why steady consistency outperforms short bursts of activity and why visibility deteriorates when coordination breaks down.

SEO AS A CAPABILITY

Organizations that treat SEO as a **continuous capability** consistently outperform those that treat it as episodic or campaign-driven. The difference is coordination.

Fragmented visibility work produces volatile outcomes. Deliberate, shared systems produce stability. Your responsibility is to create the conditions that allow SEO to operate predictably across teams: shared expectations, explicit ownership, and consistent decision logic.

SEO IN AN AI-MEDIATED WORLD

AI-mediated discovery raises the cost of ambiguity and increases the value of clarity. Systems now evaluate meaning holistically, drawing from structure, terminology, and conceptual completeness rather than surface signals alone.

From Keywords to Meaning

Search systems use semantic analysis, entity recognition, and topic modeling to assess relevance. This rewards organizations that express concepts clearly and completely, and penalizes those that rely on vague or inconsistent language.

Visibility improves when pages have a clear purpose and deliver on it. Your role is to guide teams toward reasoning about what a page must clarify for evaluators, not how it might exploit a ranking signal.

SEO AS STRATEGIC INSIGHT

Search behavior reflects how well organizational messaging aligns with evaluator expectations. It reveals competitive positioning, emerging demand, and shifts in interpretation. Managers who understand SEO treat it as a feedback loop rather than a channel.

Visibility often mirrors internal conditions. Alignment failures, rushed deployments, unstable templates, and content sprawl appear first as a decline in visibility. Improvements in process quality and coordination often appear as visibility gains before they show up elsewhere.

Visibility Signals SEO Maturity

Weak visibility frequently reflects internal fragmentation or accumulated technical debt. Strong visibility correlates with design stability, coherent messaging, and cross-functional alignment. These correlations help managers allocate attention and investment rationally.

The Economics of Visibility

Visibility reduces acquisition costs, improves conversion efficiency, strengthens brand recognition, and provides a long-term defensive advantage. It is funded through content, infrastructure, coordination, and platform stability. The economic logic is straightforward: maintained consistently, visibility produces compound returns.

STRATEGIC CHOICES IN AN AI-DRIVEN LANDSCAPE

Terminology in the industry is still evolving. Acronyms such as AEO, SGE, and GEO attempt to describe AI-mediated discovery environments. Whether these are treated as extensions of SEO or as distinct categories matters less than the shared reality: systems now evaluate meaning more comprehensively.

Clarity, terminology stability, and conceptual structure are no longer optional. They are foundational.

TYPES OF SEO

Different forms of SEO address different evaluator needs and system behaviors. Understanding these distinctions helps you prioritize work and diagnose failure modes without reverting to tactics.

Local SEO

Local visibility depends on structured business data, consistent identifiers, and accurate location signals. Structural inconsistency causes a rapid decline. Your role is to ensure alignment between content, navigation, and entity data so local interpretation remains stable.

News SEO

News visibility prioritizes freshness, source credibility, and narrative stability under time pressure. Managers support this by reinforcing predictable structures and reducing contradictory updates as stories evolve.

Image and Video SEO

Visual surfaces reinforce meaning when treated as evidential, not decorative. Consistent placement, accurate descriptions, and contextual alignment strengthen both comprehension and machine interpretation.

Enterprise SEO

At scale, visibility problems emerge from coordination failures rather than writing errors. Template drift, unmanaged variation, and unclear ownership become systemic risks. Enterprise SEO emphasizes governance, pattern stability, and predictable execution.

Ecommerce SEO

Structured, consistent product information strengthens both rankings and trust. Precision in attributes, naming, and relationships matters more than volume. Avoiding unnecessary variants protects meaning at scale.

Evergreen and B2B SEO

Evergreen content anchors authority. B2B and thought leadership visibility depend on stable definitions, coherent frameworks, and patient demonstration of expertise. Trust compounds gradually through consistency.

Support and Documentation SEO

Support-related content succeeds when the purpose is explicit and the structure is predictable. Clear task framing, strong internal linking, and early disambiguation reduce uncertainty for both evaluators and systems.

VISIBILITY COMPOUNDS

Visibility grows as content earns citations, links, recognition, and stronger entity associations. Improvements in structure and performance raise the competitiveness of every surface, not just individual pages.

VISIBILITY CHALLENGES

Most visibility failures stem from unclear ownership, fragmented processes, and competing priorities. Product teams push for speed. Marketing experiments. Engineering restructures. Legal enforces compliance. Without coordination, clarity erodes.

Your role is to keep the visibility work visible. You align responsibilities, reinforce shared language, establish review rhythms, and prevent short-term pressures from undermining long-term stability.

THE FUTURE OF VISIBILITY

Conversational interfaces, multimodal search, and generative systems will continue to reshape discovery. These systems rely on structured data, stable entities, predictable templates, and semantic clarity. Organizations that cling to outdated assumptions will struggle to remain interpretable.

THIS CHAPTER SETS THE FOUNDATION

This chapter reframes SEO as organizational clarity rather than optimization. It defines visibility as influence rather than traffic and positions managers as stewards of coherence and long-term value.

The chapters that follow build on this foundation, translating these principles into operational guidance you can apply under real constraints.

KEY PRINCIPLES IN THIS BOOK

Clarity, consistency, structure, and stability are treated as prerequisites for visibility. They are assumed rather than reintroduced. Later chapters focus on how organizations sustain these principles at scale.

FURTHER READING

- **Book 2—Accidental SEO Manager**—grounds you in the managerial responsibilities behind visibility and how to steer cross-functional work.
- **Book 4—Is Our SEO Working?**—helps you translate visibility into measurable signals you can report and improve over time.

Chapter 2

HOW SEARCH SYSTEMS INFER INTENT

Modern SEO begins with understanding why people search and what they expect to accomplish when they do. This chapter explores how search systems infer intent and how that inference shapes visibility across search results and AI-mediated surfaces. Rather than treating intent as a keyword classification exercise, this chapter frames it as a managerial lens for shaping page purpose, structure, and meaning at scale. When managers clearly understand intent, downstream decisions about content, templates, governance, and evaluation become more predictable and easier to sustain.

INTENT AS THE BASIS OF MODERN SEARCH

Search intent describes the underlying task a person is trying to complete when they use a search system. It reflects purpose rather than phrasing. People search to learn, navigate, compare, decide, or act. Search systems evaluate relevance by assessing whether a page helps complete that task, not by matching words in isolation. When content aligns with intent, users engage confidently and systems infer satisfaction. When intent is mismatched, even well-written pages struggle to perform.

Informational Intent

Informational intent covers searches where the goal is **understanding**. Users want explanations, definitions, context, or clarity. Pages that satisfy informational intent explain concepts cleanly, introduce terms consistently, and anticipate follow-up questions. These pages often anchor early stages of evaluation and shape how topics are interpreted across the rest of the site.

Navigational Intent

Navigational intent appears when **users already know what they want to reach**. They expect speed, recognizability, and confirmation. Clear labels, stable URLs, consistent titles, and strong brand signals help search systems and evaluators confirm they have arrived at the intended destination. Weak navigational signals create hesitation and misrouting even when the content quality is high.

Transactional Intent

Transactional intent reflects **readiness to act**. Users want to complete a task with minimal friction. Pages that satisfy this intent prioritize clarity, sequencing, and completion. They remove unnecessary explanation, surface decision-critical information early, and reinforce confidence. Transactional pages succeed when nothing distracts from the next step.

Commercial Investigation

Commercial investigation sits between learning and acting. Users are evaluating options, weighing trade-offs, and reducing uncertainty. Pages that serve this intent compare alternatives, explain differences, and frame decisions in practical terms. These pages often influence outcomes more than final conversion pages because they shape trust during evaluation.

HOW INTENT INFLUENCES RANKING

Search systems evaluate whether a page aligns with the task implied by the query and whether users behave as if that task was satisfied. Engagement patterns, abandonment, and progression all feed back into relevance assessment. Pages that satisfy intent consistently tend to stabilize in rankings because they demonstrate predictable usefulness. Pages that drift away from intent—even gradually—become less competitive over time.

INTENT AND ENTITIES

Entities are the **unit of reference** that modern visibility systems use to keep concepts stable. An entity may be a product, organization, service, location, policy, or concept with a distinct identity. When an entity is well-defined and consistently reinforced, it behaves like an anchor that stabilizes descriptions and relationships across the ecosystem.

Intent and entities work together. Entities help search systems understand what a page is about; intent helps determine when it should appear. When entities are described clearly and consistently, systems can match pages to a broader range of queries that express the same underlying task. Clear entity alignment improves accuracy and reduces misinterpretation, especially when users phrase queries differently.

INTENT AS A MANAGERIAL LENS

Search intent becomes powerful when it shapes decisions across teams. When managers frame planning, reviews, and prioritization around the user task, teams stop guessing and start aligning. Intent reveals where users hesitate, where explanations fail, and where pages compete unnecessarily.

Revealing User Expectations

Intent clarifies what users expect to find when they arrive. Early-stage intent reflects confusion or exploration. Mid-stage intent reflects comparison and risk reduction. Late-stage intent reflects urgency and commitment. Seeing these expectations clearly allows teams to design pages that meet demand without overloading users with irrelevant information.

Linking Intent to Business Priorities

Intent patterns map directly to business outcomes. Informational intent highlights education gaps. Commercial investigation exposes comparison friction. Transactional intent surfaces clarity or trust issues near the point of conversion. Managers use these signals to prioritize improvements where they matter most.

HOW TO DISCOVER RELEVANT INTENT

Search intent is neither guessed nor defined by SEO teams in isolation. Organizations discover the intents they must support by observing how evaluators interact with information across multiple signals and decision moments. Your role is to ensure the organization has reliable ways to surface the dominant tasks people are trying to complete.

At a managerial level, intent discovery comes from four primary sources.

Search Behavior Signals

Search data reveals recurring tasks rather than isolated keywords. Queries, refinements, and entry pages show what people are trying to accomplish before they arrive. Managers should look for clusters of behavior—questions that repeat, comparisons that recur, and actions that follow informational visits. These patterns indicate intent types that deserve durable content rather than reactive responses.

Content Performance and Engagement

Pages that consistently attract entry traffic reveal which intents the organization already serves well. Pages with high abandonment or short dwell time often signal intent mismatch rather than poor writing. Reviewing performance through the lens of task completion—rather than rankings alone—helps teams identify where expectations are unmet.

Customer and Sales Interactions

Support tickets, sales calls, onboarding friction, and customer questions often expose intent earlier than search tools do. When similar questions surface repeatedly across channels, they usually reflect an unmet informational or comparative intent that search systems will eventually amplify. Managers should ensure these signals are fed back into content planning rather than treated as isolated operational noise.

Competitive and Market Context

Competitors often reveal intent gaps indirectly. When rival pages consistently rank for comparison, evaluation, or decision-oriented queries, they signal expectations the market already has. Intent discovery here is about understanding which tasks evaluators expect someone in the market to support clearly.

Intent discovery is therefore an organizational activity, not a keyword exercise. When these signals are reviewed together, they present a stable picture of the tasks your content system must support. Later chapters show how these insights translate into content models, editorial systems, and governance—but the responsibility for recognizing intent patterns begins at the managerial level.

Your role is to ensure these intent signals are reviewed regularly and together, and translated into durable content decisions rather than reactive publishing.

INTENT AND PAGE PURPOSE

Intent becomes operational only when each page clearly states its **purpose**. Users arrive with a task, and systems test whether the page helps complete it. This is known as "satisfying the query." Pages perform best when their role is clear on the opening screenful and reinforced throughout the structure.

Making Purpose Explicit

Teams produce clearer work when the page's purpose is defined before writing begins. A simple statement—" This page exists to help the user accomplish ___"—anchors drafting, review, and revision. Purpose statements reduce debate and prevent scope creep.

Reducing Ambiguity

Pages that attempt to educate, persuade, and convert simultaneously dilute intent. Ambiguity confuses users and weakens system interpretation. Managers reinforce clarity by flagging mixed objectives, tonal shifts, and structural detours during review.

INTENT CREATES STABILITY

Pages anchored to a clear task age better. Wording, design, and examples may evolve, but purpose remains stable. Intent provides a reference point for evaluating whether changes strengthen or weaken the page over time.

Spotting Early Drift

Drift is a key concept in this book. It begins when additions no longer support the original task. Introductions expand, sections multiply, and messages blur. Managers detect drift by checking whether the opening, headings, and conclusions still serve the same user goal.

INTENT AND STRUCTURED MEANING

Knowing the intent guides content creators which entities matter most on a page and how they should be presented. When the task is informational, definitions and relationships matter most. When the task is transactional, product or service entities must be unambiguous. When the task is comparative, relationships between entities become central.

GUIDING TEAMS ON INTENT

You should ensure that all contributors share the same understanding of the purpose. Templates, briefs, editorial guidelines, and review notes should reference the intended task so decisions reinforce rather than dilute relevance.

Preventing Over-Editing

Pages often degrade through well-meaning additions. When intent is explicit, teams are less likely to add content that creates noise. Shared intent statements serve as constraints that protect clarity.

INTENT AND AI INTERPRETATION

AI systems favor pages with clear, self-contained explanations aligned to everyday tasks. When intent is explicit, pages naturally produce **liftable units** such as definitions, steps, comparisons, and summaries.

Predictable Liftable Structures

Different intents produce predictable extractable forms. Informational intent yields definitions and explanations. Commercial investigation yields comparisons and decision guides. Transactional intent yields clarifying statements and next-step cues. Clear intent improves extractability without requiring mechanical optimization.

CONNECTING INTENT AND STRUCTURE

Intent should shape the **first screenful of content**. Clear introductions, stable terminology, and focused sections signal relevance immediately. When structure aligns with the task, both users and systems interpret meaning more confidently.

The First Screenful

Search systems and AI models rely heavily on early content to infer purpose. When the opening aligns with the task, extractability improves, and abandonment decreases.

INTENT REVIEW AS GOVERNANCE

Intent becomes a governance tool when reviews begin with a single question: "Does this page still do the job it was created to do?" This reframes the evaluation from opinion to usefulness.

Three-Step Intent Review

- Purpose check: Is the task clear immediately?
- Structure check: Do sections support the task without competing goals?
- Expectation check: Does the page satisfy what a reasonable evaluator expects?

KEEPING INTENT CLEAR ACROSS TEAMS

Intent holds only when all contributors consistently reference it. Product, content, design, and engineering decisions must preserve the task the page exists to satisfy. Without shared intent, pages fragment over time.

INTENT AS THE FOUNDATION OF SEO

Intent connects how queries are interpreted, how pages are ranked, and how users decide whether to engage. When content reflects a clear understanding of the task, relevance feels immediate. Structure tightens, meaning stabilizes, and pages compete more confidently across both traditional search and AI-mediated environments.

FROM TACTICAL PILLARS TO MANAGERIAL ACCOUNTABILITY

Practitioners often describe SEO using three pillars:

- content,
- links, and
- technical execution.

That framing supports implementation but obscures managerial responsibility. At scale, these categories collapse. Content choices affect structure. Technical changes alter meaning. Linking behavior emerges from templates and governance rather than individual actions.

For managers, SEO resolves into three responsibilities:

- **Interpretability** ensures the organization's purpose, concepts, and intent are understandable to evaluators, search systems, and AI systems.
- **Structural integrity** ensures templates, navigation, and dependencies behave predictably as the site evolves.
- **Organizational control** ensures decisions move through known pathways with clear ownership and review depth. Together, these responsibilities replace tactical optimization with accountable system design.

This chapter establishes intent as the foundation of that system. Later chapters examine how intent interacts with workflows, maturity, crisis response, and long-term sustainability.

FURTHER READING

- **Book 2—Accidental SEO Manager**—strengthens your grasp of foundational concepts and how to operationalize them with teams.
- **Book 4—Is Our SEO Working?**—shows how to validate intent, purpose, and clarity using practical diagnostics.

Chapter 3

HOW SEARCH ENGINES WORK

To manage search effectively, you need a practical mental model of how search engines interpret, evaluate, and present information. This chapter explains the model at a managerial level. Rather than describing algorithms or ranking formulas, it focuses on the observable system behaviors that shape visibility: how content is discovered, how meaning is inferred, how trust is established, and how results are selected for presentation.

Search systems are not optimized for websites. They are optimized to reduce uncertainty for evaluators. Every stage of the system—from discovery to indexing to presentation—exists to answer a single question: *can this information be acted on with confidence?* When you understand search engines through that lens, many visibility outcomes become predictable.

HOW SEARCH ENGINES TREAT CONTENT

Search engines are designed to surface information that is reliable, interpretable, and appropriate to the task implied by a query, all within strict time and resource constraints. They do this by evaluating content in stages rather than indiscriminately ranking everything they find.

At a high level, search systems follow a consistent progression: they discover content, decide whether it is worth indexing, interpret its meaning, evaluate its usefulness in context, and select an appropriate representation. Each stage acts as a filter. Content that creates uncertainty, ambiguity, or redundancy is progressively deprioritized.

Because the internal mechanics are opaque, effective management does not depend on knowing algorithms. It depends on recognizing stable system tendencies. Across search platforms, the same patterns recur: content that is easy to discover, clearly declares its purpose, uses consistent terminology, and maintains structural coherence is more likely to be indexed. Content that is ambiguous, duplicative, slow, or internally inconsistent is more likely to be ignored or suppressed.

From a managerial perspective, outcomes matter more than implementation. Pages are either discovered or overlooked, indexed or excluded, interpreted consistently or misclassified, promoted or deprioritized. These outcomes reflect how well the site communicates meaning under automated evaluation.

DISCOVERY AND CRAWL RELIABILITY

Search engines discover content by following links, sitemaps, and previously known URLs. Discovery reliability depends less on submission mechanisms and more on predictable site behavior.

Internal linking is the primary discovery signal. Links establish relationships between pages and indicate relative importance. Broken links, orphaned pages, excessive variants, inconsistent navigation, and pagination traps all weaken crawl coverage and distort the system's understanding of site structure.

Sitemaps act as discovery hints rather than guarantees. When they accurately reflect the site's conceptual structure, they help orient crawlers efficiently. When they are bloated, outdated, or misaligned with internal linking, they lose influence and are deprioritized in favor of crawl-derived signals.

Discovery problems are rarely isolated technical issues. They usually reflect structural disorder: unclear hierarchies, uncontrolled variation, or navigation patterns that obscure relationships between pages.

INDEXING AS AN EVALUATIVE DECISION

Search engines do not index everything they discover. Indexing is selective and reflects an algorithmic judgment about whether a page provides distinct, interpretable value.

Pages are excluded when they duplicate nearby material, lack substance, load poorly, or fail to communicate a clear purpose. Common causes include thin pages, overlapping variants, inconsistent definitions, outdated templates, and weak internal linking that fails to establish relevance within the site.

At a system level, indexing reflects trust in coherence. Sites with stable templates, consistent purpose signals, and controlled variation are indexed more reliably. Fragmented signals reduce confidence and lead to selective exclusion.

In practical terms, a page effectively does not exist in search systems until it is indexed. Stable indexing is the prerequisite for ranking, presentation, and reuse across surfaces.

INTERPRETING MEANING

I said at the start that "meaning" is an important concept in modern search. Before ranking occurs, search engines attempt to understand what a page is *about* and what role it plays. Interpretation relies on language, structure, definitions, and relationships between pages.

Clear purpose statements, coherent headings, stable terminology, and alignment between intent and content all reduce classification uncertainty. When pages contradict themselves—through mixed objectives, shifting definitions, or fragmented structure—systems must guess. Guessing lowers confidence and limits reuse.

Semantic models further assess topics, entities, and relationships to stabilize interpretation across contexts. When entities are described consistently, and relationships are reinforced through internal linking, meaning becomes easier to preserve even when content is excerpted or summarized.

Interpretation is therefore not a ranking concern; it is a prerequisite for reliable ranking and presentation.

RANKING IN CONTEXT

Ranking orders interpreted pages by estimated usefulness for a given query. Systems weigh multiple signals, including intent alignment, content depth, structural coherence, historical performance, and evidence of real-world utility.

Ranking is contextual. Results vary by intent, location, device, and prior behavior. Two evaluators may see different rankings for the same query because the system is optimizing for relevance within their respective contexts.

For managers, this means rankings are not absolute indicators of success or failure. Movement reflects how well pages perform *for specific tasks*, not how well they conform to a universal order.

PRESENTATION AND REUSE

After interpretation and ranking, search engines select presentation formats that minimize effort and uncertainty for evaluators. Links, snippets, panels, maps, and AI-generated summaries are different representations drawn from the same evaluative model.

Pages with a clear purpose, stable structure, and ordered information are safer to extract from. They are more likely to appear in snippets, summaries, or generative frames because meaning survives partial reuse. Pages with ambiguous structure or mixed objectives are less likely to be lifted prominently and more likely to be misrepresented when they are.

Presentation reflects confidence. The clearer the meaning, the more assertively the system will reuse it.

QUALITY AS A SYSTEM PROPERTY

Search engines protect result quality to preserve trust. Quality assessment evaluates patterns across pages rather than isolated signals.

Clusters with inconsistent depth, structure, or definitions indicate systemic weakness and reduce confidence across the site. Thin content, manipulative tactics, or fragmented meaning quickly erode trust. Sites that control variation, maintain consistent standards, and preserve purpose across updates are treated as more stable over time.

Quality risk increases during redesigns, migrations, and content expansions. Organizations that manage these transitions deliberately—by preserving structure and meaning—recover more reliably.

THE ROLE OF HUMAN RATERS

Human quality raters contracted by Google do not determine rankings directly; instead, their assessments inform how Google calibrates its quality models. Rater guidelines emphasize clarity of purpose, depth and accuracy, supporting evidence, and alignment with user expectations.

These evaluations reinforce system definitions of reliability and usefulness. Over time, they shape what the system learns to trust and reuse. Understanding this role helps managers explain why clarity, evidence, and consistency matter even when no immediate ranking change is visible.

In Google's quality framework, these judgments are organized under Experience, Expertise, Authoritativeness, and Trustworthiness (E-E-A-T), which together describe how confidently a system can rely on a source when extracting or reusing its content.

MANAGING SEARCH AS A SYSTEM

Search engines reward sites that behave predictably under evaluation. When structure holds, purpose is clear, and meaning is stable, visibility becomes easier to sustain.

This chapter provides the system model. Later chapters translate these principles into operational controls: how to design content that clearly declares intent, how to maintain structural integrity as sites scale, how to govern change without destabilizing meaning, and how to diagnose failures when visibility declines.

Search does not reward cleverness. It rewards clarity that survives scale.

FURTHER READING

- **Book 2—Accidental SEO Manager**—simplifies how search platforms discover, crawl, and evaluate pages so you can explain system behavior clearly to non-technical stakeholders.
- **Book 4— Is Our SEO Working?**—expands on indexing, discovery patterns, evaluator interpretation, and how movement signals connect to reporting frameworks you can use.

Chapter 4

THE NEW SEARCH LANDSCAPE

Search no longer occurs within a single, unified environment. Discovery now spans platforms, applications, assistants, and vertical systems, each interpreting information according to its own logic and incentives. Visibility must therefore be understood across an **ecosystem of surfaces** rather than measured solely by rankings or traffic.

This chapter explains how modern discovery environments differ, why visibility fragments across them, and what that fragmentation means for managerial decision-making. The goal is to understand the forces that shape exposure, interpretation, and trust across a diverse landscape.

FROM A SINGLE RESULTS PAGE TO AN ECOSYSTEM OF SURFACES

The traditional search engine results page (SERP) is no longer the sole entry point for discovery. Modern search unfolds across many surfaces that users move between fluidly, often without recognizing where one form of discovery ends and another begins.

People encounter information while scrolling social feeds, browsing marketplaces, navigating maps, or using everyday phone apps. These encounters shape awareness and preference long before a formal query is entered. Discovery increasingly begins upstream of search engines, even when it eventually passes through them.

This shift has not made discovery more complex so much as more representative of real behavior. Users do not think in terms of platforms; they think in terms of tasks. Systems now compete to reduce effort at each step of those tasks.

FROM RETRIEVAL TO INTERPRETATION

Many modern platforms prioritize interpreted answers over lists of links. Structured facts, summaries, comparisons, and guided explanations increasingly appear directly within interfaces, allowing users to assess options without visiting source sites.

This change shifts discovery from document retrieval toward meaning extraction. Visibility now depends on whether information can be interpreted safely and presented confidently, not merely whether it can be retrieved.

When content clearly declares its purpose, uses stable terminology, and preserves meaning when excerpted, it is easier for systems to reuse. When structure is weak, or intent is mixed, systems reduce prominence or avoid reuse altogether.

DISCOVERY WITHOUT QUERIES

Discovery no longer requires explicit queries. Recommendation systems embedded in everyday platforms infer intent from behavior rather than keywords.

Music, video, and retail platforms surface content based on prior engagement. Mapping tools introduce nearby services based on context. Social feeds expose products, ideas, or explanations that users did not actively seek. These systems shape what users consider before intent becomes explicit.

For managers, this means visibility often precedes demand. Early impressions form through exposure rather than search, influencing which queries are later issued and which brands feel familiar or credible.

THE DECLINE OF UNIFORM RESULTS

Context-dependent, **personalized** outputs have replaced uniform search results. Results now vary by location, device, history, subscriptions, and platform context.

Two people issuing the same query may see different answers because systems are optimizing for relevance within individual contexts rather than enforcing a universal ranking. This variability is intentional. It reflects a shift toward guidance rather than standardization.

Managers should therefore treat rankings as situational signals rather than absolute measures of performance.

THE AI-MEDIATED SEARCH ENVIRONMENT

The modern search ecosystem includes multiple AI-enabled systems that combine indexing, retrieval, and generative reasoning in different proportions. Google, Bing, Perplexity, and specialized assistants each define usefulness differently, producing divergent results for similar topics.

Some systems emphasize continuity with traditional indexing, layering generative elements cautiously. Others foreground guided reasoning, comparison, or conversational framing. Still others blend retrieval with explicit source citation.

These environments operate as semi-independent systems rather than a unified network. Visibility depends on how each defines interpretability, safety, and usefulness.

PLATFORM INCENTIVES AND BUSINESS MODELS

Business models shape discovery behavior. Advertising-supported platforms optimize for engagement and satisfaction. Marketplaces prioritize pricing, availability, fulfillment reliability, and return risk. Subscription platforms emphasize depth and consistency. Recommendation-driven environments rank content based on interaction signals.

These incentives explain why the same information may surface differently across platforms. Visibility outcomes reflect platform priorities rather than inconsistencies in underlying facts.

Understanding incentives allows managers to anticipate where clarity matters most and where commercial or behavioral signals dominate.

INDUSTRY AND CONTEXTUAL VARIABILITY

Discovery patterns differ by industry because users gravitate toward platforms aligned with category-specific decision needs.

Travel discovery concentrates on aggregators that emphasize availability and policy constraints. Job discovery aligns with role- and seniority-based platforms. Local services surface through mapping tools optimized for proximity and status. Retail discovery concentrates on marketplaces optimized for fulfillment.

These category-aligned surfaces often shape perception before general search engines are involved. Visibility is therefore contextual rather than universal.

GEOGRAPHIC AND REGULATORY DIFFERENCES

Search and AI systems adapt to local language, regulation, and dominant digital ecosystems. Privacy requirements, compliance standards, and regional platform preferences influence how information is ranked and presented.

As a result, visibility varies by country even when content remains unchanged. Differences often reflect regulatory sensitivity or platform dominance rather than shifts in user demand.

Managers should interpret international visibility through the regional context rather than assuming global uniformity.

HOW PLATFORMS CONSTRUCT VISIBILITY

Each platform constructs visibility using models shaped by its priorities and constraints. Some emphasize structured entity relationships, others behavioral signals, and others commercial performance.

Independent data stores, ingestion pipelines, and quality controls limit interoperability. A business may appear consistently in one environment and inconsistently in another because each system maintains its own representation of the company.

Cross-platform discrepancies are therefore a normal outcome of independent modeling, not necessarily a signal of failure.

APP-CENTRIC AND FRAGMENTED JOURNEYS

Discovery journeys now unfold across fragmented touchpoints. Users move between apps, devices, and platforms, often encountering the same organization in different contexts before forming a decision.

Visibility accumulates across systems without consistently producing immediate visits. Influence may occur through recognition, familiarity, or trust long before a click is recorded.

This fragmentation challenges attribution but reflects how modern discovery actually works.

TRUST, VERIFICATION, AND BRAND SIGNALS

AI systems rely on **trust signals** to reduce the risk of misrepresentation. Consistency across sources, corroboration by recognizable entities, and stability over time increase confidence.

Commercial platforms prioritize verified data and review patterns. Sensitive domains emphasize provenance and compliance. AI assistants favor established brands because they reduce uncertainty when generating explanations.

Brand coherence, therefore, functions as a visibility amplifier across systems, even when direct optimization is limited.

GOVERNANCE, EXPOSURE, AND CONTROL

Organizations must decide how much exposure they allow across AI-mediated systems. Allowing AI crawlers enables participation in generative summaries and assistants that shape early discovery. Restricting access reduces reuse risk but limits visibility.

Some organizations experiment with mechanisms such as the *llms.txt* file to signal preferences to AI crawlers, but these files function as governance declarations rather than enforceable controls. They document intent, risk posture, and participation boundaries, yet offer no guarantees of compliance. As such, they should be treated as policy artifacts—helpful for alignment and accountability—but not relied upon as technical safeguards.

These realities make governance decisions strategic rather than technical.

MANAGING VISIBILITY IN A DIVERSE SYSTEM

As discovery systems proliferate, visibility depends less on platform-specific optimization and more on alignment. Stable terminology, coherent descriptions, and predictable structure reduce ambiguity across independent environments.

Visibility is shaped by decisions made across content, marketing, operations, legal, and customer experience teams. When coordination breaks down, inconsistencies spread across platforms that interpret inputs independently.

Managing the modern search landscape, therefore, requires cross-functional awareness, disciplined governance, and an acceptance that visibility is distributed rather than centralized.

This chapter explains *where* discovery happens and *why* it fragments. Later chapters address *how* organizations maintain coherence, control risk, and sustain visibility across this evolving ecosystem.

FURTHER READING

- **Book 3—AI Visibility Playbook**—frames AI-mediated discovery, llms.txt decisions, and governance for emerging surfaces.
- **Book 2—Accidental SEO Manager**—helps you translate landscape shifts into practical direction without chasing hype.

Chapter 5

THE SYSTEM BEHIND SEARCH VISIBILITY

WHY VISIBILITY IS SYSTEMIC

Search visibility does not emerge from isolated optimizations or individual publishing decisions. It is the result of how definitions, structures, evidence, and workflows behave together across an organization. When those elements reinforce one another, meaning stays stable, and performance becomes more predictable. When they drift independently, visibility weakens even if individual pages appear well executed.

A common misconception is that visibility can be fixed one page at a time. Page-level improvements matter, but their impact depends on the environment in which they operate. If definitions shift upstream, templates evolve unevenly, or structured information becomes inconsistent, even strong pages struggle to anchor meaning. Managers gain leverage when they treat **visibility as an operational system**, because systemic problems stop reappearing under new forms.

HOW SYSTEMS CREATE MEANING

Meaning is created collectively. A single page may carry an explanation, but many teams influence the conditions that shape how that explanation is understood and trusted. Over time, the organization becomes legible through repeated signals: stable definitions, predictable structures, consistent attributes, and reliable update pathways. When those signals align, the organization appears coherent. When they contradict each other, the system's confidence declines.

What Strong Systems Have in Common

Strong visibility systems share a few recognizable traits across industries:

- Definitions remain stable across functions and channels
- Similar page types follow predictable structures
- Attribute data aligns across pages, structured data, and external listings
- Evidence and source-of-truth information is easy to find and consistently referenced
- Changes propagate through known pathways rather than personal memory

These traits create an environment where clarity moves through the organization without relying on individual interpretation.

HOW WEAK SYSTEMS FAIL

Weak visibility systems rarely collapse suddenly. They erode through minor inconsistencies that compound over time. A terminology change applied in one region does not reach others. A template revision updates only part of a section. A feature release changes the user journey but does not trigger supporting updates. Each variation seems minor, but together they create a pattern of instability.

Over time, that instability produces outcomes leaders experience as unpredictable: performance fluctuations, reduced eligibility for prominent representations, and increased effort required to maintain consistency. Users also notice contradictions between product behavior, marketing claims, and support explanations long before dashboards make the problem obvious.

Early Signs of Drift

System drift becomes visible internally before it becomes measurable externally. You will often see:

- Repeated questions about terminology and definitions
- Slower review cycles as teams validate meaning manually
- Debates about decisions that previously felt straightforward
- Support teams flagging recurring discrepancies in rules, thresholds, or workflows
- Increased exceptions and one-off edits to "patch" clarity

These signals indicate the system is no longer holding meaning together and needs reinforcement.

MEANING LIVES IN CLUSTERS

Meaning rarely resides on a single page. Users navigate clusters of interconnected pages—definitions, explanations, comparisons, troubleshooting guidance, and supporting evidence—that together shape understanding of a topic. Search systems interpret clusters similarly. A canonical page often carries the primary explanation, while supporting pages confirm, extend, and stabilize that meaning.

Clusters allow organizations to express complex subjects with nuance and depth. They also expose system weaknesses quickly. When cluster behavior becomes inconsistent, the signal weakens even if individual pages read well in isolation.

Why Cluster Consistency Matters

Consistency across clusters strengthens meaning by signaling reliability. When terminology aligns, structural patterns repeat, and evidence appears in predictable locations, interpretation becomes easier and less risky. Users benefit from more precise navigation and fewer contradictions. Internally, teams benefit because they inherit patterns rather than reconstruct them for each new page.

ENTITIES AS OPERATIONAL ASSETS

How Entities Become Strong

An entity strengthens when:

- It has a canonical definition and preferred name
- The definition appears consistently across key page types
- Attributes match across visible content and structured information
- Related concepts link back to it predictably
- Competing descriptions do not dilute its meaning

Entity strength comes from consistent, governed reinforcement across the places where people and systems expect to find the same facts.

Alignment across Channels

External platforms also shape entity confidence. Listings, knowledge panels, reviews, product feeds, directories, and regulatory references contribute to the entity's broader representation. When these sources align with canonical descriptions, visibility strengthens. When they contradict one another, confidence declines, and representation becomes less stable.

FRAGMENTATION AND DRIFT

Fragmentation weakens visibility by scattering meaning across overlapping pages, outdated variants, and inconsistent explanations. Drift is the common mechanism behind fragmentation. Drift occurs when definitions or descriptions change unintentionally across pages, templates, or updates. Minor variations introduced over time accumulate into ambiguity that undermines confidence.

Common Organizational Causes

Drift typically emerges from predictable behaviors:

- Contributors rewriting existing definitions in their own style
- Legacy pages contradicting newer explanations
- Regional variants diverging from canonical terminology
- Template changes altering meaning unevenly across clusters
- Product or policy updates failing to propagate to dependent pages

Each introduces interpretive noise. Over time, the system becomes less certain which version reflects the organization's intent.

Stabilizing the Canonical Meaning

Preventing fragmentation requires a clear source of truth. Canonical pages should anchor:

- The most precise definition and scope boundaries
- Complete and stable attribute sets
- Terminology that remains fixed across channels
- Structured information aligned with visible facts
- Explicit links to dependent pages and variants

Dependent pages should support the canonical explanation rather than reinterpret it. Regional, seasonal, or campaign-specific content should reference the canonical page instead of restating core definitions.

COHERENCE UNDER CHANGE

Organizations that sustain coherence treat meaning as an operational asset rather than a documentation task. They centralize definitions so every contributor starts from the same anchor. They protect structural patterns during high-change periods, ensuring that hierarchy, workflow sequences, and evidence placement remain reliable. They make update pathways predictable so teams know how changes should propagate.

Keeping Definitions Current

Definitions must evolve as products and policies change, but that evolution must be controlled and visible. When a definition changes in one area but not another, it means fractures, e.g. "major incident", "sensitive personal data."

Users encounter contradictory thresholds and rules. The system is uncertain which version reflects the current intent. Mature organizations ensure contributors find the current definition first, not a legacy version buried in older assets.

Managing Structural Changes

Structural changes—template updates, component revisions, navigation shifts, layout refinements—carry outsized impact because structure conveys meaning. A change in hierarchy alters what appears most important. A change in module order reshapes the task flow. A partial rollout creates inconsistent interpretation across otherwise similar pages. Effective systems sequence structural updates deliberately and verify that meaning remains intact across the surfaces that matter.

REDUCING VARIABILITY ACROSS TEAMS

Variability is a primary source of internal inconsistency. Different teams create similar pages with other structures, terminology, and evidence placement. Each variation may seem harmless, but together they create interpretive noise that is costly to maintain. Reducing variability does not constrain creativity. It protects meaning by establishing a stable baseline.

Structural Alignment

Similar page types should follow similar structures. When they do not, users must relearn patterns, and teams must re-decide basic layout logic on every update. Predictable structures allow contributors to focus on the substance of the explanation rather than improvising format decisions. They also make governance simpler because changes can be evaluated against known expectations.

E-E-A-T AND TRUST SIGNALS

Search platforms invest heavily in distinguishing credible information from content that is merely well written. Google refers to this trust-oriented lens as Experience, Expertise, Authoritativeness, and Trustworthiness (E-E-A-T.)

E-E-A-T isn't a single ranking factor you can "optimize." It is a set of quality expectations that shape how quality raters evaluate whether information can be relied on, reused, and surfaced with confidence—especially in sensitive topics or high-stakes decisions.

E-E-A-T is easiest to manage when treated as an operational standard rather than a content guideline. Experience shows that when your organization demonstrates real-world knowledge of the scenario it describes, not just abstract definitions. Expertise shows when explanations are accurate, complete, and technically sound for the audience. Authoritativeness grows when reputable sources corroborate your claims and when your organization is consistently recognized for the topic. Trustworthiness is the outcome of disciplined accuracy: stable terminology, clear ownership, consistent facts, and prompt correction when something changes.

In practice, E-E-A-T is reinforced through repeatable choices: who is accountable for critical pages, how facts are sourced and updated, how credentials are represented, how policies and specifications are kept consistent across surfaces, and how the organization prevents drift. That is why evidence belongs in a system model of visibility. Evidence is one of the most concrete ways to translate E-E-A-T from a quality concept into a governed practice.

EVIDENCE AS THE ANCHOR

Evidence is one of the most practical ways to reinforce E-E-A-T, because it grounds explanations in verifiable sources rather than interpretation or memory. Users trust guidance more readily when its basis is clear. Organizations also maintain consistency more effectively when contributors work from the same references.

Matching Evidence to the Task

Evidence should align with the page's job. Decision support may require worked examples or explicit criteria. Rule explanations may require authoritative references or explicit scope. Comparisons require consistent attribute sets and transparent trade-offs. Troubleshooting requires validated steps and known outcomes. When evidence matches the task, comprehension improves and ambiguity declines.

Updating Evidence at the Right Pace

Evidence decays when it does not keep pace with change. Outdated specifications, legacy thresholds, or superseded policies introduce uncertainty, undermining trust. Strong systems retire stale references, refresh proofs on a known cadence, and ensure teams encounter current sources first.

SCALING MEANING ACROSS THE ORGANIZATION

Organizations struggle to scale visibility when meaning depends on individual memory. As teams grow and content volumes increase, minor variations multiply faster than editorial review can correct them. Scaling meaning reduces the cognitive effort required to produce accurate work by embedding clarity into the system.

Automation as Reinforcement

Automation does not replace expertise. It reinforces it by detecting deviation earlier than manual review can. Automated checks can flag missing attributes, inconsistent terminology, structural omissions, schema mismatches, and template drift before problems reach users. This reduces silent degradation and keeps variance from becoming systemic.

Lowering Cognitive Load

High cognitive load increases variability. When contributors face unclear expectations, they improvise, and improvisation introduces drift. Lowering cognitive load means reducing discretionary decisions that create risk. Templates, canonical definitions, and clear decision rules guide contributors even under time pressure. When contributors inherit clarity rather than reconstruct it, meaning scales reliably.

OWNERSHIP AND ESCALATION

Ownership stabilizes meaning by making accountability explicit. When definitions, structures, and evidence lack owners, changes propagate unevenly, and teams apply local interpretations that conflict with system coherence. Ownership is a safeguard, especially in high-impact areas.

High-Impact Areas

Not every page requires tight control, but some categories carry disproportionate risk: regulated topics, core workflows, key product specifications, canonical definitions, and foundational templates. These areas should have named owners, defined change criteria, and escalation pathways, as errors spread quickly and are costly to reverse.

Authority to Enforce Standards

Ownership without authority is ineffective. Owners need the ability to reject changes that introduce ambiguity, require supporting evidence, coordinate multi-surface updates, and pause releases when meaning is at risk. This is how governance moves from advisory to operational.

MAKING STABILITY THE DEFAULT

Strong visibility outcomes are usually the consequence of stable systems, not heroic individual effort. When definitions are centralized, structures are predictable, evidence is visible, and ownership is clear, teams make consistent decisions without constant oversight. Over time, clarity becomes the default output of everyday work.

This chapter establishes the system model: meaning is reinforced through coordinated signals, maintained through predictable patterns, and protected through governance. Later chapters translate this model into practical operating rhythms, content systems, and quality controls that make the system durable.

FURTHER READING

- **Book 3—AI Visibility Playbook**—offers system-level guardrails for meaning, patterns, and ownership.

- **Book 2— Accidental SEO Manager**—turns system thinking into day-to-day management behaviors.

Chapter 6

BUILDING A MATURITY MODEL FOR VISIBILITY

Visibility becomes predictable when an organization can produce consistent outcomes at scale. Without maturity, improvements decay: one team fixes terminology while another reintroduces drift; performance work in one area is offset by regressions elsewhere; a redesign disrupts structures that previously supported interpretation. A maturity model lets you diagnose these inconsistencies as system conditions, not isolated mistakes, and prioritize the changes that move the organization toward repeatable performance.

THE FIVE LEVELS OF ORGANIZATIONAL MATURITY

The five levels of organizational maturity introduced in these books are inspired by Carnegie Mellon University's Capability Maturity Model (CMM) or its successor, CMMI (Capability Maturity Model Integration), whose model for software capability has the following levels:

1. Initial
2. Managed
3. Defined
4. Quantitatively Managed
5. Optimizing

Website governance requires different labels, but the same premise applies: maturity describes system reliability, not individual effort.

Organizations rarely sit at a single maturity level across all visibility domains. That unevenness is often the real cause of "mysterious" volatility—one domain behaves predictably while another introduces contradictions, regressions, or incomplete signals.

Level 1—Ad Hoc

Level 1 work is improvised. Definitions live in personal memory, contributors solve local problems without seeing downstream effects, and similar pages drift into inconsistent structures. Accessibility and structured data are handled inconsistently, performance degrades as assets accumulate, and measurement is mostly retrospective because ownership is unclear. Outcomes depend on individuals, so gains are fragile.

Level 2—Emerging

Level 2 begins when teams recognize repeat problems as inconsistency, not isolated defects. Basic term lists, a few protected templates, and ad hoc safeguards reduce obvious errors, but the fixes do not generalize across clusters. Structured data improves in pockets, measurement becomes more informative, and AI surfaces may represent some areas accurately while misreading others. Work is less chaotic, but reliability is still uneven.

Level 3—Structured

At Level 3, structure is standardized. Templates and page-type patterns constrain variation, so similar intents are expressed in similar ways across large page sets. Accessibility and performance are planned into delivery rather than treated as remediation. Structured data follows maintained schemas, and measurements support diagnosis at the template and cluster levels. The organization can produce consistent outputs across a defined scope, even if cross-domain alignment is incomplete.

Level 4—Integrated

Level 4 is cross-domain coherence. Content, design, engineering, product, measurement, accessibility, and compliance operate from shared assumptions about page types, dependencies, and change impact. Decisions are coordinated early, reducing downstream conflict and rework. Measurement is used to reconcile trade-offs across domains rather than interpreted in isolation. The system remains stable through regular change cycles because dependencies are visible and managed.

Level 5—Optimized

Level 5 is continuous control. Drift is detected early, fixes follow known paths, and regressions are prevented through automation and disciplined change practices. Canonical sources are maintained as operational assets, templates survive redesigns without structural breakage, and performance and accessibility stay stable through feature work. The organization's default behavior is correction before small inconsistencies become systemic volatility.

MATURITY MODELS ACROSS DOMAINS

Organizations can be Level 4 in one domain and Level 2 in another. The result is a mixed system: some signals remain stable while others introduce contradictions. The practical value of a maturity model is identifying which domain is capping overall reliability and which improvements will change system behavior rather than producing isolated wins.

Content Governance

Low maturity shows up as shifting definitions, overlapping intents, and revisions that change meaning without coordinating dependent pages. Higher maturity shows stable topic boundaries, consistent terminology across clusters, and updates that propagate deliberately.

Template and Architecture Governance

Low maturity leads to template drift: similar page types express information differently, and partial rollouts create inconsistent structures for the same intent. Higher maturity produces stable page-type patterns and controlled template evolution across large inventories.

Performance Governance

Low maturity is reactive: regressions appear after releases, and optimizations are local rather than sustained. Higher maturity keeps performance stable through change because budgets and constraints are enforced consistently across templates and components.

Accessibility Governance

Low maturity treats accessibility as cleanup, leading to inconsistent semantics and interaction patterns. Higher maturity produces predictable interaction behavior and durable semantic structure across page types, improving consistency across devices and assistive contexts.

Measurement Governance

Low-maturity measures outcomes without isolating causes, so teams debate interpretations and react late. Higher maturity uses stable indicators tied to templates, clusters, and workflows, making it easier to attribute and compare change impacts over time.

AI and Extractability Governance

Low maturity produces inconsistent summaries because entities, relationships, and page structures vary across clusters. Higher maturity produces a stable representation because core concepts are expressed consistently and reinforced across dependent content.

Contract Governance

Low maturity treats external work as an add-on and accepts deliverables that do not match internal patterns, increasing drift risk. Higher maturity defines expectations that align partner output with internal page types, data practices, and change coordination.

ADVANCING THROUGH THE MATURITY LEVELS

Maturity typically advances through targeted changes that remove recurring failure modes. The goal is to improve repeatability: fewer exceptions, fewer one-off structures, and fewer local interpretations that conflict with the rest of the system.

From Level 1 to Level 2

The transition from Level 1 to Level 2 focuses on arresting chaos rather than improving quality. Teams begin by documenting baseline definitions, identifying high-risk pages or templates, and replacing purely ad hoc decisions with minimal shared rules. The objective is to reduce dependency on individual memory so that work does not collapse when contributors change or pressure increases.

From Level 2 to Level 3

Moving from Level 2 to Level 3 requires formalizing patterns that were previously applied inconsistently. Templates, page types, and content boundaries become explicit and repeatable rather than selectively protected. Performance and accessibility expectations are defined upfront, and structured data shifts from one-off fixes to maintained schemas. This transition reduces rework by ensuring contributors inherit structure rather than manually reconstructing meaning.

From Level 3 to Level 4

The shift from Level 3 to Level 4 is driven by integration rather than additional structure. Domains that previously operated independently—content, engineering, design, analytics, compliance—begin coordinating decisions using shared assumptions and awareness of dependencies. Changes are evaluated for downstream impact before release, reducing conflicts and stabilizing outcomes across clusters rather than resolving issues locally after delivery.

From Level 4 to Level 5

Advancing from Level 4 to Level 5 focuses on resilience in the face of change. Reinforcement mechanisms—automation, monitoring, and disciplined review—detect drift early and correct it predictably. Canonical sources, templates, and constraints are maintained as operational assets, allowing the system to absorb redesigns, staffing changes, and regulatory updates without losing reliability.

FURTHER READING

- **Book 2—Accidental SEO Manager**—explains how to build capabilities stepwise and sustain them across teams.
- **Book 4—Is Our SEO Working?**—maps maturity to metrics so you can evidence progress credibly.

Chapter 7

THE ZERO-CLICK CHALLENGE

Search visibility increasingly unfolds in environments where users receive answers without visiting a website. These zero-click experiences change how information is discovered, interpreted, and reused, even when your content never generates a session. Understanding this dynamic allows managers to evaluate performance more accurately and guide their organizations toward strategies that remain effective as interfaces continue to evolve.

In this chapter, "systems" refers to the combined retrieval, ranking, knowledge, and generative components that produce zero-click answers—not language models in isolation.

UNDERSTANDING ZERO-CLICK BEHAVIOR

Zero-click behavior emerges when search engines and AI systems resolve user intent within the interface itself. Users receive the answer immediately as a synthesized explanation, a structured comparison, or a conversational response. They do not need to click a link to complete the task, because the system has already assembled the relevant information from trusted sources. This shift has transformed visibility from an output of ranking to an outcome of interpretation. Your goal is to make your content reusable, stable, and unambiguous so systems can incorporate it confidently.

How Systems Reuse Content

Modern systems **assemble meaning** rather than deliver pages. They extract definitions, map relationships between entities, identify authoritative examples, and recognize patterns across pages. When your content offers stable terminology, clear boundaries, and predictable structures, models reuse it without hesitation. Reuse does not always generate traffic, but it creates influence—your explanations shape the narrative even when sessions do not rise.

Drivers of Zero-Click Behavior

Zero-click behavior accelerates as search platforms compete to resolve user tasks with minimal effort and delay. AI-mediated interfaces accelerate this trend by summarizing information in conversational formats that eliminate the need for clicking blue links altogether. The more models improve at synthesizing information, the more frequently users receive complete answers without having to click through. As a result, visibility becomes a measure of how often your content is reused upstream rather than how users usually arrive downstream.

The Role of Stable Meaning

Visibility in zero-click environments depends on whether systems can reuse your explanations without hesitation. When terminology shifts, definitions vary, or structures change unpredictably, platforms cannot determine which version of your position is correct. Uncertainty reduces reuse.

Stable meaning allows systems to carry explanations forward across queries, refinements, and conversational turns. When an answer is reused confidently, it becomes part of the platform's working knowledge rather than a one-off response. This continuity matters because zero-click experiences often unfold over multiple interactions, not a single query.

Organizations that maintain stable meaning are reused more often, more accurately, and across more surfaces. Those that do not are sampled inconsistently or excluded entirely—not as a penalty, but as a risk-avoidance choice by the system.

HOW ZERO-CLICK AFFECTS MANAGERS

Zero-click environments force managers to rethink how visibility is evaluated and how success is communicated. The traditional relationship between search impressions, clicks, and onsite conversions no longer holds linearly. You want to guide your organization toward a more accurate understanding of where influence occurs and how users complete their journeys. Managers who adapt early gain clarity, secure better funding, and avoid the cycle of explaining declining traffic year after year. The challenge is to shift internal expectations from a page-centric worldview to a system-centric one—where content becomes a reusable knowledge asset rather than a destination.

Visibility without Traffic

Visibility now occurs upstream, before users decide whether a click is necessary. Your content may appear in featured snippets, comparison elements, local modules, product cards, or generative summaries without producing a measurable session. This does not diminish its strategic value. Zero-click visibility often guides decision-making directly within the interface. A user may select a product, refine a query, choose a store, or compare services without visiting any website that shapes the answer.

Measuring Influence

Influence reflects how often your explanations participate in the pathways users rely on. It captures a broader and more accurate picture of visibility in an ecosystem where models synthesize meaning. Influence includes being cited in summaries, appearing in conversational responses, providing attributes for entity panels, and stabilizing definitions that LLMs reuse. These signals indicate how deeply your organization shapes user understanding. Managers who focus on influence produce strategies aligned with the real behavior of modern systems rather than outdated traffic metrics.

Communicating Performance

Stakeholders often equate declining clicks with declining performance. You want to reframe this assumption by showing that clicks are only one of many outcomes in a landscape where tasks are completed earlier and more efficiently. Success now includes representation across formats, consistency in entity attributes, stability in canonical definitions, and inclusion in synthesized explanations. When stakeholders see success as influence rather than traffic, they make better investment decisions and support initiatives that strengthen long-term visibility.

PREPARING YOUR ECOSYSTEM

Zero-click environments reward organizations that maintain clarity, structure, and consistency across their entire ecosystem. Preparation is an ongoing discipline. The more coherent your ecosystem becomes, the more confidently platforms can reuse your content across AI Overviews, conversational answers, and synthesized summaries. Preparation allows you to compete in an environment where machines—not users—perform the first round of interpretation.

MANAGING ZERO-CLICK OVER TIME

Zero-click environments are not a temporary shift. They will continue evolving as search engines refine how they summarize information and as AI systems become more capable of reasoning across sources. Managing zero-click over time means building habits that prevent drift, maintain clarity across teams, and ensure that your organization remains a dependable source of truth for both users and machines.

Monitoring Changes in Representation

Representation patterns shift as platforms adjust their models, introduce new surfaces, or refine the criteria used to populate answer formats. You need to monitor how often your explanations appear in summaries, conversational responses, or structured modules. Declines in representation do not always signal failure—they may reflect platform-wide rebalancing. Still, monitoring these shifts provides early warnings when clarity weakens or when competitors establish momentum. By watching representation trends, you can intervene before visibility losses compound.

Maintaining Definition Stability

Definition stability influences how platforms treat your content. You want definitions that remain consistent across channels, pages, and updates. When teams rephrase definitions or adjust terminology without coordination, systems detect conflicting signals. This weakens reuse and reduces trust in your material. Maintaining stable definitions requires transparent governance, established ownership, and disciplined review practices. When stability becomes routine, your organization retains authority as interfaces evolve.

Adapting without Creating Drift

Adaptation is necessary, but unmanaged adaptation introduces drift. You want change processes that preserve meaning while allowing templates, evidence, and examples to evolve. Each update should reinforce your conceptual model rather than erode it. This balance becomes increasingly important as generative systems rely on long-term patterns. Adaptation succeeds when teams modify details while protecting the core structure that makes your content reliable.

FURTHER READING

- **Book 2—Accidental SEO Manager**—shows how to redefine success and influence when clicks decline.
- **Book 4—Is Our SEO Working?**—provides ways to measure representation, lift, and brand effects without traditional traffic.

Chapter 8

DIGITAL MATURITY AND ORGANIZATIONAL READINESS

DEFINING DIGITAL MATURITY

Digital maturity determines how far your organization can progress in visibility work before internal friction, workflow gaps, or capability limitations slow momentum. When maturity is low, even straightforward visibility initiatives become difficult to execute. When maturity is high, improvements compound because teams understand the system, make decisions confidently, and prevent drift before it escalates.

Digital maturity is measured by how consistently your teams translate visibility intent into visibility outcomes. You assess maturity by evaluating execution patterns, decision-making behaviors, cross-functional alignment, workflow stability, and the organization's ability to maintain clarity as it scales.

High maturity produces predictable movement, low regression risk, and strong evaluator experiences. Low maturity leads to hesitation, inconsistency, reactive behavior, and a constant need for corrective work. Your task is to recognize its presence—or absence—clearly enough to act on it.

RECOGNIZING MATURITY SIGNALS

If maturity determines how far you can go, signals reveal where you actually stand. Every organization leaves clues about its level of digital maturity. Some appear in how teams communicate; others surface in how consistently work is executed under pressure.

Mature organizations show consistency. They make decisions using shared definitions, align work across functions, and rely on predictable workflows that reduce ambiguity. Immature organizations struggle with coordination, rely on individual heroics, and drift into instability because teams interpret the exact requirements differently.

Your goal is to read these patterns accurately. Maturity signals do not diagnose individual performance; they expose system behavior. Once identified, they allow you to focus improvement efforts where they will have the greatest effect.

Alignment Signals

Alignment signals reveal how well **teams** coordinate decisions that influence visibility. When alignment is strong, teams anticipate dependencies, escalate uncertainty early, and resolve conflicts before they become regressions. Requirements flow smoothly, and templates behave predictably across teams.

Weak alignment shows up as conflicting assumptions, contradictory priorities, or incomplete handoffs. Recurrent regressions, inconsistent structural patterns, and tension between product expectations and technical realities indicate readiness gaps that no amount of execution effort can overcome.

Workflow Signals

Where alignment reflects coordination, workflows reveal operational reality. Mature environments rely on stable processes that reduce confusion and eliminate unnecessary variation. Immature environments rely on informal communication, shifting expectations, and unstable release cycles, leading to template and content drift.

Workflow maturity becomes visible by observing how work moves from intake to completion. Incomplete requirements, fragile handoffs, frequent regressions, or bypassed governance are not isolated failures; they are indicators of readiness constraints that must be addressed before scale is possible.

Decision Signals

Decision-making signals show how confidently teams operate within the system. High-maturity teams make decisions using shared principles, escalate risk early, and apply patterns consistently across the ecosystem.

Low-maturity teams hesitate, reopen decisions repeatedly, or defer responsibility until issues become urgent. When decision signals weaken, visibility performance fluctuates because consistency cannot be sustained across releases.

BUILDING FOUNDATIONAL READINESS

Once signals are visible, the next step is strengthening the conditions beneath them. Foundational readiness determines whether your organization can maintain stability while making progress. Before introducing advanced visibility frameworks, teams must understand the system, use shared definitions, and collaborate predictably.

Readiness is built through documentation and repeated reinforcement of expectations and patterns. When teams understand why structure matters—not just how to follow it—they adopt visibility practices with greater confidence and consistency.

Establishing Shared Language

Shared **language** is the first readiness milestone. When teams use consistent terminology to describe signals, templates, scenarios, or evaluators, interpretation becomes easier, and collaboration accelerates.

Without shared language, every conversation becomes a negotiation. Different definitions for the same concept introduce friction, rework, and uneven execution. Consistent terminology stabilizes decisions across functions before governance is required to intervene.

Clarifying Ownership

Language alone is insufficient without accountability. **Ownership** determines who decides, who executes, and who maintains stability over time. Mature organizations define ownership explicitly; immature ones distribute it vaguely.

When ownership is unclear, drift accelerates because no one feels responsible for template consistency, narrative alignment, or workflow stability. Clarifying ownership reduces regression risk by making stewardship visible and expected.

Strengthening Communication

With ownership established, **communication** determines execution quality. Predictable rhythms—regular reviews, structured escalation paths, and consistent check-ins—ensure signals are interpreted correctly, and misalignment is corrected early.

Communication maturity often improves readiness faster than any other factor because it reduces surprise. When teams know when and how issues surface, they act with greater confidence and coordination.

UNDERSTANDING CAPABILITY GAPS

Even aligned, well-communicating teams encounter limits. Capability gaps determine how much complexity your organization can absorb before instability appears. These gaps are not signs of failure; they reflect normal organizational evolution.

As visibility environments become more complex, the capability required to support them increases. The management task is to identify which gaps threaten stability and which merely slow progress.

Technical Capability Gaps

Technical gaps involve template behavior, rendering consistency, structured data accuracy, device performance, and architectural fragmentation.

Addressing them requires clarifying expected patterns and guiding teams toward implementation models that behave predictably across environments.

Narrative Capability Gaps

Narrative gaps emerge when evaluator needs are misunderstood, framing varies across similar pages, or explanations lack clarity.

These gaps are reduced by reinforcing scenario mapping, narrative alignment, and governance practices that support consistency at scale.

Process Capability Gaps

Process gaps appear when workflows stall, handoffs fail, or responsibilities overlap.

Strengthening intake patterns, governance routines, and decision cycles often delivers disproportionate gains because process maturity stabilizes everything built on top of it.

READINESS FOR AI-INTERPRETED SYSTEMS

Capability gaps become more visible in AI-interpreted environments. As generative systems reuse content aggressively, organizational maturity increasingly determines whether explanations are represented accurately.

LLMs reward consistency, clarity, and structure because these qualities reduce ambiguity. Organizations that behave predictably—through stable templates and coherent definitions—are easier for AI systems to interpret and reuse.

Low-maturity organizations emit contradictory signals that reduce confidence and exposure. High-maturity organizations benefit from compounding effects as coherence strengthens representation across interfaces.

NAVIGATING CULTURAL BARRIERS

Structural readiness can be undermined by culture. Digital maturity is both technical and depends on how people perceive responsibility, governance, and accountability.

Resistance often manifests as role deflection, diluted ownership, or fear of scrutiny. Addressing these barriers requires treating measurement as diagnostic support rather than criticism and aligning incentives with system-level success rather than local optimization.

ELEVATING LEADERSHIP READINESS

Cultural signals ultimately reflect leadership readiness. Executives who understand dependencies, drift patterns, and structural fragility make more durable decisions.

Leadership readiness improves when visibility is understood as a **system capability shaped by engineering, content, governance, and operations**—not as a switch that can be toggled on demand. When leaders internalize this model, priorities stabilize, and maturity rises across the organization.

SCALING MATURITY AT PACE

Once foundational readiness is established, scale introduces a new constraint. Growth tests whether shared patterns can survive onboarding, turnover, and parallel execution across teams.

Scaling maturity requires reinforcing what must remain consistent while allowing controlled variation elsewhere. Organizations that define non-negotiables clearly maintain coherence without sacrificing agility, enabling growth without regression.

FURTHER READING

- **Book 5—The C-Suite Blind Spot**—connects maturity signals to leadership behaviors and resourcing.
- **Book 2—Accidental SEO Manager**—turns readiness gaps into practical, staged capability building.

Chapter 9

PERFORMANCE, SPEED, AND USER EXPERIENCE

PERFORMANCE AS AN INTERPRETIVE CONDITION

Website performance influences visibility before relevance, authority, or ranking signals are evaluated. Systems cannot interpret what they cannot access reliably, and users cannot trust what feels unstable. Speed, stability, and responsiveness, therefore, act as preconditions for meaning rather than optimizations layered on top of it.

When performance is weak, interpretation degrades quietly. Pages may still rank, and content may still exist. But systems hesitate. Rendering is incomplete, relationships are harder to infer, and extraction confidence declines. Performance failures rarely announce themselves as visibility failures, which is why they are often underestimated.

Performance is a signal of operational reliability.

WHY SPEED SHAPES UNDERSTANDING

Speed determines when meaning becomes available. Both users and machines begin forming judgments almost immediately after a page starts loading. Delays interrupt comprehension and distort prioritization.

A slow page does not simply arrive late. It arrives fragmented. Key elements appear out of sequence, headings lose their anchoring role, and definitions may surface after context has already been misread.

Systems encounter the same problem. When rendering is delayed or staggered, they struggle to determine which elements are foundational and which are supplementary.

Speed, therefore, affects interpretation directly. It controls the order in which meaning is revealed.

Early Elements Carry Disproportionate Weight

The first elements rendered on a page—titles, headings, summaries, primary navigation—anchor interpretation. When these load quickly, systems gain confidence. When they load late, systems guess.

This is why performance issues often manifest as misclassification rather than outright exclusion. The content exists, but its role is misunderstood.

LATENCY AS STRUCTURAL FRICTION

Latency, defined as the delay between a request and a usable response, introduces friction at every stage of discovery. For users, it interrupts flow. For systems, it increases processing cost.

Search engines and AI systems adapt to latency by reducing how often they engage in deep processing. Crawl frequency declines. Rendering shortcuts are taken. Pages that consistently perform poorly become less attractive candidates for reuse, especially in synthesized or generative contexts where efficiency matters.

Reducing latency is therefore not about pleasing impatient users. It is about lowering the cost of interpretation.

Infrastructure Choices Become Visibility Decisions

Server response times, caching behavior, and geographic distribution determine how quickly content becomes available to interpret. Website infrastructure typically combines the content management system with server-side platforms and, in many cases, a content delivery network. These components are often procured and managed separately, yet each can independently improve or degrade performance.

These are not neutral engineering choices. Slow infrastructure delays indexing updates, weakens freshness signals, and increases the likelihood that systems rely on cached or partial representations of your content. In international contexts, poorly distributed infrastructure creates uneven visibility that is difficult to diagnose solely from analytics.

Infrastructure sets the ceiling for every other performance improvement.

RENDERING ORDER AND MEANING

Rendering a web page is a sequence of events. That sequence matters.

When scripts block rendering, stylesheets delay layout, or frameworks inject content late, the page presents meaning in pieces. Systems attempting to extract structure encounter incomplete hierarchies and shifting relationships. Users experience similar confusion, even if they cannot articulate it.

Performance improvements that prioritize rendering order—deferring non-essential scripts, simplifying CSS, and eliminating unnecessary dependencies—are interpretive. They allow meaning to appear whole rather than assembled gradually.

Mobile Environments Expose Weak Assumptions

Mobile performance reveals architectural shortcuts quickly. Limited bandwidth, variable hardware, and constrained screens amplify every inefficiency.

Because mobile surfaces increasingly mediate AI-assisted discovery, mobile performance now influences visibility across all platforms, not just handheld devices. A page that performs adequately on desktop but poorly on mobile sends mixed signals about reliability.

Optimizing for mobile conditions is no longer optional. It is the baseline for interpretability.

STABILITY MATTERS AS MUCH AS SPEED

Fast pages that behave unpredictably still undermine trust. Stability determines whether meaning remains intact after it appears.

Layout shifts, injected elements, and late-loading media disrupt comprehension. Users lose their place. Systems lose confidence in hierarchy. Even small shifts introduce ambiguity about which elements matter most.

Layout Stability Preserves Hierarchy

Stable layouts protect meaning by ensuring that what appears first stays first, and what anchors the page remains anchored. Reserving space for media, defining dimensions explicitly, and avoiding post-render rearrangement all contribute to interpretive clarity.

Stability allows systems to learn patterns and reuse them reliably.

MEDIA AS A PERFORMANCE RISK

Media is often the largest source of performance degradation and instability.

Unoptimized images delay rendering. Autoplay media interrupts the flow. Heavy assets strain devices unevenly. These issues affect users immediately and systems indirectly by delaying access to core content.

Media should support explanation, not compete with it. When media behavior is intentional—responsive sizing, compression, and deferred loading—it reinforces meaning rather than obscuring it.

PERFORMANCE AND INTERPRETATION AT SCALE

AI systems do not interpret intent from static HTML alone. They interpret **rendered output**.

If performance issues delay or fragment rendering, extraction becomes unreliable. Headings may be missed. Lists may be incomplete. Relationships between elements may not be recognized at all. A slow page can still rank. But it is less likely to be reused.

Extractability Depends on Early Clarity

AI systems favor sources they can process efficiently. Pages that reveal their structure quickly are easier to summarize, segment, and recombine.

Delayed scripts, complex frameworks, and client-side rendering introduce uncertainty. Systems may choose alternative sources simply because they are easier to interpret, not because they are more authoritative.

Performance, therefore, influences whose explanations shape the narrative.

MULTI-SURFACE PERFORMANCE EXPECTATIONS

Visibility now spans surfaces with very different constraints: mobile apps, conversational interfaces, embedded summaries, and voice responses.

A page that works in one context may fail in another. Voice interfaces may never capture headings that load late. Content hidden behind interactions may be invisible to extraction systems.

Performance models must anticipate these surfaces. When pages behave consistently across contexts, systems treat them as safe inputs.

GOVERNING PERFORMANCE OVER TIME

Scripts accumulate. Features expand. Exceptions proliferate. One-time optimization projects fail because they do not change behavior. Long-term performance requires ownership, lifecycle integration, and routine evaluation.

Governance ensures that performance remains a constraint, not an afterthought.

Ownership Prevents Invisible Regression

When no one owns performance, everyone assumes someone else is watching it.

Clear ownership across engineering, product, and SEO ensures that performance risks surface early. Ownership turns performance from a reactive fix into a planning consideration.

Embedding Performance into Delivery

Performance should be evaluated before code is written, not after it ships.

When teams consider performance during design and planning, they choose simpler interactions, lighter dependencies, and clearer structures. When they do not, performance becomes expensive to recover later. This reduces rework and preserves interpretive clarity.

MONITORING WITHOUT OVERREACTING

Performance monitoring should focus on patterns rather than panic. Sustained degradation, repeated instability, or widening gaps between environments signal structural issues that warrant attention.

Diagnostics are most valuable when they surface trends early enough to act calmly.

PERFORMANCE AS ORGANIZATIONAL DISCIPLINE

Performance is a habit. Organizations that treat it as a shared responsibility maintain clarity more easily than those that treat it as a technical specialty.

When engineering, design, product, and content teams understand how performance affects interpretation, decisions align naturally. Complexity is questioned. Exceptions are justified. Stability becomes cultural rather than enforced.

Performance supports long-term visibility through consistent restraint.

FURTHER READING

- **Book 3—AI Visibility Playbook**—embeds performance, stability, and accessibility into governance rhythms.
- **Book 4—Is Our SEO Working?**—links performance to observable outcomes and ongoing monitoring.

Chapter 10

CONTENT ARCHITECTURE AND INFORMATION HIERARCHY

This chapter assumes that dominant intent patterns have already been identified using the organizational signals outlined in Chapter 2

WHY STRUCTURE DETERMINES VISIBILITY

Visibility does not emerge from individual pages acting alone. It appears from how pages relate to one another, how intent is signaled through **structure**, and how consistently meaning is expressed across an ecosystem. Content architecture is the system that holds those relationships together. When it is coherent, search engines and AI systems can interpret your domain with confidence. When it is inconsistent, even strong content becomes harder to classify, reuse, or trust.

Site architecture is an interpretive framework. Search and AI platforms infer expertise by observing how ideas are grouped, how hierarchy is applied, and how reliably similar concepts behave across pages. Your architecture teaches systems what matters, what is foundational, and what is merely supportive.

Poor architecture does not usually fail loudly. It fails **quietly**. Signals weaken, clusters blur, and pages begin competing with one another for the same interpretations. Managers often misdiagnose this as a content quality issue when the underlying cause is structural.

ARCHITECTURE AS A MEANING SYSTEM

Content architecture exists to express **meaning at scale**. It does this by constraining variation and reinforcing patterns that systems learn to trust. When structure is predictable, platforms stop guessing.

A page does not explain itself in isolation. Its role is inferred from where it sits, how it is framed, and what surrounds it. Architecture gives that context. It tells systems whether a page defines a concept, supports a decision, compares options, or resolves a task. Without that context, interpretation becomes probabilistic rather than confident.

This is why architecture matters more as your content footprint grows. Small sites can survive on intuition. Large ecosystems cannot. Once dozens or hundreds of contributors are involved, meaning must be enforced through structure rather than memory.

Structure Signals Intent before Content Is Read

Before a system processes your words, it processes your structure. Headings, hierarchy, internal links, and page roles all act as pre-interpretive signals.

When those signals are consistent, systems learn quickly. When they vary, systems hesitate. Hesitation reduces reuse, weakens summarization, and increases the likelihood that competitors with clearer structures will be preferred in synthesized results.

Structure answers three questions immediately:

- what this page is for
- how it relates to nearby pages
- how much authority it should carry

If those answers are unclear, the content itself must work harder—and often fails to compensate.

DESIGNING A HIERARCHY THAT REFLECTS THOUGHT

Hierarchy concerns whether heading levels reflect the conceptual weight of their content.

Many sites flatten the hierarchy unintentionally. Everything becomes an H2. Every detail is elevated to structural importance. The result is noise. Systems struggle to distinguish anchors from elaboration, and AI summaries often extract the wrong statements because the hierarchy does not reflect meaning.

A proper hierarchy does some things well:

- It establishes a clear conceptual entry point
- It separates the core explanation from the supporting detail
- It preserves a stable ordering across similar pages

Hierarchy should mirror how a human would explain the topic aloud, not how a CMS happens to organize fields.

Sequencing Information to Reduce Ambiguity

Sequence is part of the hierarchy. Ideas introduced too early might confuse. Ideas introduced too late could fail to anchor meaning.

Effective sequencing follows a reliable progression:

- define the concept or task
- establish why it matters or how it is used
- introduce variations, constraints, or examples

When this sequence is stable across a cluster, systems detect pattern reinforcement. When it varies, pages begin competing for different interpretations of the same intent.

Sequence **discipline** is one of the simplest ways to improve visibility without changing a single sentence of copy.

CLUSTERS AS THE BACKBONE OF ARCHITECTURE

Clusters are not collections of related URLs. They are expressions of how your organization understands a topic.

A strong cluster has:

- a clear conceptual center
- predictable supporting page roles
- stable internal linking that reinforces hierarchy

Clusters fail when they reflect internal ownership rather than user logic. Search engines and AI systems do not care which team owns a page. They care whether the pages together express a coherent mental model.

When clustering is done well, several things happen naturally. Maintenance becomes easier. Redundancy declines. Updates propagate more safely. Visibility stabilizes because systems encounter the same relationships repeatedly.

Preventing Intra-Cluster Competition

One of the most common architectural failures occurs when pages compete within the same cluster. This happens when boundaries are unclear, and roles overlap.

Competition weakens interpretation. Systems receive mixed signals about which page is authoritative, which is explanatory, and which is supplemental. Over time, all pages in the cluster underperform.

Clear clustering prevents this by making the page's purpose explicit. Each page exists to do one job. Architecture enforces that separation long before content quality becomes a factor.

TEMPLATES AS ARCHITECTURAL ENFORCEMENT

Page templates are not productivity tools first. They are **enforcement** mechanisms.

A template encodes decisions about:

- where meaning appears
- what must be present
- what cannot be improvised

When templates are stable, contributors no longer have to make structural decisions repeatedly. This is how meaning scales without supervision.

Poor templates invite variation. Contributors fill gaps differently, introduce new sections opportunistically, and rearrange content to suit local needs. Over time, this erodes the architectural signals that systems rely on.

Stabilizing Page Purpose through Template Design

Every template should make the page's purpose obvious before a word is read.

That purpose is reinforced by:

- consistent opening structures
- fixed locations for definitions or summaries
- predictable placement of supporting elements

When the page purpose is stable, systems classify more confidently. AI models reuse content more accurately because the role of each page is unambiguous.

Templates that allow too much freedom do not empower contributors. They shift architectural responsibility onto individuals, which guarantees drift at scale.

NAVIGATION AS INTERPRETIVE GUIDANCE

Navigation is how architecture becomes visible. It shows users and systems how ideas connect and which paths matter.

Good navigation reflects user tasks, not internal structures. It prioritizes conceptual proximity over organizational charts. When navigation mirrors how people think, interpretation improves across every surface—search, AI summaries, assistive technologies, and internal discovery.

Navigation problems often masquerade as content problems. Users loop. Systems misclassify. Pages isolate. The fix is rarely more content. It is clearer pathways.

Predictability over Exhaustiveness

Navigation does not need to expose everything. It needs to be predictable.

Predictable navigation:

- uses consistent labels
- preserves category boundaries
- avoids sudden structural shifts

When movement is predictable, systems learn faster. They identify hubs, understand depth, and infer authority more reliably. Predictability reduces interpretive costs, thereby increasing reuse.

PRESERVING ARCHITECTURE OVER TIME

Architecture decays unless it is actively maintained. New pages are added. Old ones are repurposed. Exceptions accumulate.

Preservation does not require a heavy process. It requires clarity about what must not change.

That usually includes:

- cluster boundaries
- page roles
- heading behavior
- template regions

When these elements are protected, the system absorbs growth without losing meaning.

Updating Structure without Breaking Meaning

Architecture must evolve, but updates should be surgical. Large **restructures** introduce risk because they ripple across clusters and templates simultaneously.

Safer updates:

- adjust one layer at a time
- validate impact on related pages
- preserve established patterns unless there is strong evidence to change them

When updates reinforce existing logic rather than replace it, systems continue to trust the structure they have already learned.

DESIGNING FOR FUTURE CONTRIBUTORS

Architecture succeeds when future contributors cannot easily break it.

This is about reducing the number of decisions that require judgment. When structure is enforced through templates, navigation, and hierarchy, contributors focus on expressing meaning rather than inventing form.

Future-proof architecture:

- limits improvisation
- encodes intent
- survives turnover

When that happens, visibility becomes durable. Not because every page is perfect, but because the system itself remains interpretable.

FURTHER READING

- **Book 3—AI Visibility Playbook**—supports architecture decisions, structural guardrails, and change control.
- **Book 2—Accidental SEO Manager**—helps you align structure with user tasks and keep contributors coordinated.

Chapter 11

STRUCTURED DATA AND ENTITY CLARITY

This chapter moves from architectural intent to enforceable meaning declarations.

STRUCTURED DATA AS A MEANING CONTRACT

You do not implement structured data to "add SEO." You implement it to **lock meaning in place**. It is a **contract** between the page, your systems, and the interfaces that interpret you. When the contract is coherent—text, structure, and markup all pointing to the same thing— search engines and large language models treat your content as easier to reuse. When the contract is inconsistent, they do not "punish" you; they hedge. They pull less from you, cite you less, and prefer sources that cost less to interpret.

Structured data does not rescue unclear pages. It makes it easier to trust clear pages at scale. That distinction keeps teams from wasting effort polishing markup while leaving the underlying intent unresolved.

START WITH THE SINGLE PAGE CLAIM

Before you discuss schema types, ask what claim the page is making. Not "what keywords does it target," but what it represents. A page that tries to be a definition, a comparison, a purchase funnel, and a troubleshooting guide will never produce stable signals, no matter how good the markup is. The fastest way to improve your structured data posture is to enforce a single primary page purpose.

Once the claim is fixed, structured data becomes straightforward. You no longer have to guess whether the entity is a product, service, process, organization, or event. You are confirming it.

The First-Paragraph Test

If a page's opening cannot state, in plain language, what the page is and who it is for, you should treat the schema work as premature. The opening is the human version of the same contract that the schema is trying to formalize. When the opening is fuzzy, markup becomes a costume.

This is where managers add value. You do not write the code. You force the page to be decisive about what it is.

CHOOSE THE ENTITY, THEN CHOOSE THE SCHEMA

Teams often pick a schema type because they saw it in a tool or a competitor's source code. That reverses the sequence. The entity comes first. Schema follows.

A practical way to make this non-negotiable is to require an explicit entity decision in briefs. If the entity cannot be named, the page cannot be marked up responsibly. That single habit prevents a surprising amount of downstream drift.

Entity Boundaries

Most meaning failures are **boundary failures**. A "service" page becomes a hybrid of service and pricing policy. A "product" page absorbs troubleshooting content. A "how-to" page quietly turns into a category landing page. The schema then amplifies the confusion by confidently declaring the wrong thing.

You prevent this by treating page boundaries as part of governance. The page can link out to adjacent tasks, but it should not absorb them.

DEFINE A STABLE ATTRIBUTE SET

Examples of attributes: SKU, brand, color, size, availability, price, and so on.

Once the entity is clear, you need a stable set of attributes that will be true next week, next quarter, and after the next redesign. If the organization cannot reliably maintain an attribute, it does not belong in your "meaning contract." It will become a future contradiction.

This is where many implementations fail. Teams add fields because they can. Later, someone changes a label, a range, or a format in one system and forgets the others. The unchallenged markup becomes a record of yesterday's truth.

Fewer Fields, Better Signals

A smaller, more accurate attribute set is more valuable than an ambitious one that drifts. Your objective is minimum contradiction. When you treat structured data as a stability discipline, you naturally favor attributes that are owned, maintained, and testable.

If you want teams to internalize this, measure the rate of schema corrections over time. A high correction rate indicates that the attribute set is too fragile.

ESTABLISH ONE SOURCE OF TRUTH

Your website is rarely the only system publishing meaning. Product feeds, location databases, documentation portals, support articles, and internal APIs all emit descriptions. Search engines see all of it. They do not care which team owns which platform.

You reduce inconsistency by declaring one source of truth for each core attribute and then forcing everything else to inherit from it. That can be a database, a content model, or a controlled page type. The detail does not matter. The hierarchy does.

Prevent "Parallel Descriptions"

Parallel descriptions are where drift multiplies: a feed says one thing, a landing page says another, the markup says a third. The organization thinks it has "versions." Search engines see contradictions.

You stop this by requiring each attribute to have a single upstream owner and a single format. When teams want to introduce a new representation, they must justify the need and demonstrate inheritance. Otherwise, they are creating a future repair job.

PUT STRUCTURED DATA UNDER CHANGE CONTROL

Schema breaks most often during routine work: template tweaks, component swaps, localization, CMS migrations, and "small" redesigns. This non-malicious failure is invisible until the platform stops reusing you.

Treat schema as a release artifact. If a template change ships, the schema must be validated in the same release. If a feed mapping changes, the schema must be validated as part of the same change ticket. This is basic operational hygiene.

The Minimal Gate

You do not need a complex committee. You need one predictable gate that teams cannot bypass:

- confirm the entity
- confirm the stable attribute set
- confirm markup matches the rendered page

- confirm the change did not create contradictions across similar pages

If you want a single phrase for teams to remember, use this: do not ship new meaning without confirming the meaning contract.

TREAT VALIDATION AS AN OPERATIONAL LOOP

Validation is not a one-time check or a launch-phase activity. It is an operational loop that runs whenever your system changes, answering a simple question: does the system still say what leadership intends it to say, in a form that external systems can reliably interpret?

At a basic level, validation requires code and markup to conform to recognised standards, so that pages are syntactically correct and machine-readable. Tools can confirm that markup meets specification, but that is only the starting point.

Automated validation catches structural and syntax errors. The most expensive failures, however, are semantic—the code is valid, yet the meaning no longer matches the page, or the page no longer matches the cluster it belongs to.

For that reason, you need two kinds of validation. One checks correctness: whether the code conforms to standards and functions as specified. The other checks coherence: whether meaning, structure, and intent remain aligned as content, templates, and policies evolve.

Coherence Checks

Coherence checks are simple questions asked repeatedly:

- Does this page still represent the same entity it represented last month?
- Do similar pages express the same attributes in the same order and format?

- Did a template change, relocate meaning-critical sections?
- Did a regional variant introduce a competing definition?

These checks prevent drift from becoming a slow-moving reputation leak. You are not chasing a scoring tool. You are protecting interpretability.

USE STRUCTURED DATA TO SUPPORT REUSE, NOT JUST RANKING

In zero-click environments, representation matters as much as sessions. Structured data can make your content easier to extract into summaries, panels, and conversational answers, but only if the underlying meaning is coherent. When your markup reinforces stable page claims and stable attributes, systems can safely lift your information without guessing.

This is how you keep structured data in its proper role. It is an explicit, maintained declaration of what your content means.

POSITIONING STRUCTURED DATA IN THE ARCHITECTURE STACK

Structured data is a confirmation layer that validates intent already made clear through structure, hierarchy, and narrative. When teams treat schema as additive, they create a parallel meaning system that can drift independently. When they treat it as confirmatory, structured data stabilizes interpretation.

This is why structured data belongs immediately after performance and architecture. Performance ensures meaning is rendered in time to be interpreted. Architecture ensures meaning is organized predictably. Structured data then reinforces that interpretation rather than attempting to manufacture it.

Position schema discussions inside architectural reviews, not post-launch SEO checklists. When teams understand that markup reflects architectural intent, they stop asking which schema types to deploy and start asking whether the page's meaning is sufficiently resolved to declare at all.

BOUNDARIES OF STRUCTURED DATA USAGE

Structured data is strongest when constrained. Over-declaration weakens confidence by increasing the surface area for inconsistency. Pages that attempt to enumerate every possible attribute often signal uncertainty, especially when those attributes cannot be maintained across releases, regions, or variants.

Guide teams toward meaning sufficiency rather than coverage. Search systems prefer a small number of durable signals over an expansive set that drifts. This is particularly important for evolving products, loosely bounded services, and conceptual content where definitions change over time.

Not every page benefits from a structured declaration. Exploratory analysis, narrative explanation, and opinion-led content often gain more from clarity in prose and hierarchy than from formal markup. Forcing schema into these contexts can flatten nuance and introduce false precision.

If a page's purpose cannot be summarized cleanly in one sentence, it is not ready for structural declaration. The schema should follow resolution, not attempt to create it.

ORGANIZATIONAL RESPONSIBILITY AND DECISION RIGHTS

Structured data failures rarely originate in markup syntax. They originate in ownership gaps. When no one is clearly accountable for meaning consistency, the schema becomes fragmented by default.

Engineering implements what is requested. Content teams write what is needed locally. SEO attempts to reconcile conflicts after they are already visible to systems.

You reduce this risk by assigning **responsibility** at the **meaning level**, not the implementation level. Someone must own the definition of the entity being declared, the attributes that matter, and the conditions under which those attributes may change. This role is often overlooked because it does not map neatly to existing job titles, but it is essential for durability.

Decision rights should be explicit. Teams should know who can approve changes to declared meaning, who must be consulted when attributes shift, and which pages act as anchors for broader interpretation. Without this clarity, schema updates become reactive and inconsistent, even when everyone involved is competent.

Structured data governance succeeds when teams agree that changing meaning is a higher bar than changing presentation.

MANAGING CHANGE WITHOUT CREATING INTERPRETIVE SHOCK

Meaning systems react poorly to sudden, widespread shifts. Even accurate updates can destabilize interpretation if they propagate too quickly across the ecosystem. Search systems evaluate not only what changes, but how coordinated and sequential those changes appear.

Sequence updates deliberately. Anchor pages move first. Supporting pages follow once definitions stabilize. Structured data should lag narrative updates slightly, not lead them. This allows systems to detect continuity rather than contradiction.

During rebrands, mergers, or product restructures, resist the urge to update everything simultaneously. Temporary incompleteness is less damaging than conflicting signals. Meaning that evolves in phases is interpreted as intentional; meaning that shifts everywhere at once is interpreted as noise.

EVALUATING STRUCTURED DATA THROUGH AN INTERPRETIVE LENS

Validation tools answer whether markup is valid, not whether it is trustworthy. A page can pass every technical check and still weaken visibility if its declared meaning conflicts with adjacent content or parallel pages.

Shift evaluation toward interpretive questions:

- Does this declaration reinforce what the page already makes obvious?
- Would the meaning remain clear if the markup were removed?
- Do similar pages declare the same concepts in compatible ways?

This reframes review from compliance to confidence. Tools remain useful for error detection, but conceptual alignment requires human judgment. When teams adopt this posture, structured data becomes quieter—fewer declarations, each carrying more weight.

CLOSING THE LOOP WITH ARCHITECTURE AND PERFORMANCE

Structured data does not compensate for architectural ambiguity or unstable performance. It amplifies existing conditions. Clear architecture becomes clearer. Weak structure becomes more visible. Stable meaning compounds; fragile meaning degrades faster.

For this reason, structured data must be reviewed alongside architecture and performance, not in isolation. When all three reinforce each other, systems encounter a coherent signal environment. When one lags, the others cannot fully compensate.

The long-term advantage lies in alignment rather than optimization. Organizations that treat structured data as part of a broader meaning system produce signals that remain legible as interfaces evolve. Durability—not markup completeness—is the true return.

FURTHER READING

- **Book 3—AI Visibility Playbook**—deepens your understanding of how AI systems interpret structure, evaluate clarity, and reuse organizational explanations.
- **Book 4—Is Our SEO Working?**—strengthens your ability to connect structured data, extractability, and machine-interpretation signals to measurable performance outcomes.

Chapter 12

ACCESSIBILITY & INCLUSIVE DESIGN

ACCESSIBILITY FOUNDATIONS

Accessibility relies on widely recognized standards and stable principles that guide how digital experiences should behave. These foundations help your teams build predictable interfaces, reduce ambiguity, and support users who navigate with assistive technologies or alternative input methods. They also give search engines and AI models a clearer structure to interpret, which strengthens your visibility. You want your organization to internalize these foundations because they provide the shared language and stable expectations that make accessibility sustainable across contributors, releases, and redesigns.

WCAG and Global Standards

The central reference for accessibility is the Web Content Accessibility Guidelines (WCAG), maintained by the World Wide Web Consortium (W3C) and used globally by regulators, procurement teams, and accessibility auditors. WCAG defines how interfaces should behave so that people using assistive technologies—such as screen readers, magnifiers, switch devices, and voice input—can navigate and understand your content. **Most organizations aim for WCAG 2.2 Level AA** because it balances feasibility with meaningful impact. This version strengthens expectations around touch targets, focus visibility, consistent help mechanisms, and cognitive load, reflecting how real users interact with modern mobile interfaces and applications. A new framework, WCAG 3.0, is in development and moves toward more flexible scoring and broader inclusion, signaling a future in which accessibility is measured by user experience as much as by technical compliance.

Conformance Levels

WCAG defines three levels of conformance that give managers a practical sense of scope. Level A removes the most severe barriers and establishes a baseline that prevents outright exclusion. Level AA is the standard expected for most public-facing organizations and covers the issues that most frequently block tasks for users with disabilities. Level AAA represents the highest standard and is typically feasible only for specific content types or controlled environments. You want teams to understand these levels because they influence procurement requirements, redesign priorities, and long-term governance. Conformance levels set expectations not only for what should be fixed, but also for how quickly teams must act when barriers appear.

Principles That Guide Accessibility

Behind every version of WCAG sit four stable principles: content must be perceivable, operable, understandable, and robust (POUR). These principles help you evaluate whether barriers are structural, behavioral, or content-related. Perceivable experiences use sufficient contrast, clear structure, and meaningful alternatives. Operable experiences support keyboard navigation and predictable interaction patterns. Understandable experiences avoid ambiguity and reduce cognitive load. Robust experiences behave reliably across assistive technologies and changing devices. These principles give managers a practical lens for evaluating accessibility during redesigns, component updates, content reviews, and QA cycles. They turn accessibility into a durable practice rather than a checklist activity.

LEGAL AND REGULATORY EXPOSURE

Global Obligations

Different regions impose different rules, but the direction is consistent: accessibility is mandatory. In the United States, the Americans with Disabilities Act (ADA) remains the basis for most digital-accessibility claims, and case volume continues to rise across ecommerce, SaaS, hospitality, and financial services. In the European Union, the Web Accessibility Directive governs public-sector sites, while the European Accessibility Act expands requirements across industries. Canada's AODA, the UK's Equality Act, and Australia's Disability Discrimination Act similarly position accessibility as a civil-rights obligation. These frameworks converge on the same benchmark: WCAG 2.2 Level AA. When your content, templates, or components fail to meet this baseline, you risk investigations, demand letters, or litigation. Even small inconsistencies expose your organization if they block essential tasks for users with disabilities.

Common Failure Points

Most legal complaints focus on predictable, preventable issues. A button that lacks an accessible name, a form field without a label, a menu that cannot be opened with a keyboard, or a video without captions—all of these break tasks for assistive-technology users. Many organizations assume accessibility failures must be complex, but most originate in simple oversight rather than deep technical defects. These failures occur because teams rely on visual testing, move quickly under deadlines, or treat accessibility as an afterthought. When patterns drift across templates, components, and content, barriers accumulate quietly until users confront them. Recognizing these failure points early allows you to prevent issues before they generate legal exposure.

Reducing Risk through Transparency

An accessibility statement does not eliminate liability, but it reduces exposure by demonstrating good faith and documenting progress. You want your statement to articulate your standards, acknowledge known gaps, outline planned improvements, and commit to responsible timelines. Courts and regulators look for transparency because it signals seriousness and intent. When your accessibility statement is visible, accurate, and updated regularly, it strengthens your case that accessibility is a continuous practice rather than a reactive response. This transparency also helps users understand what to expect, reducing the likelihood that frustration will escalate into formal complaints.

ESTABLISHING AN ACCESSIBILITY BASELINE

You cannot improve what you cannot see. Before setting goals, commissioning audits, or building roadmaps, you want an honest view of your **current accessibility posture**. Most organizations discover that accessibility is inconsistent—some templates behave predictably, others contain structural flaws, and content quality varies by contributor. A baseline gives you clarity and prevents teams from making assumptions about accessibility based solely on visual usability. Establishing this baseline sets the stage for systematic, sustainable improvement rather than reactive fixes or rushed compliance efforts.

Lightweight Early Assessments

You can learn a surprising amount from three simple exercises: run an automated scan across high-traffic templates, navigate core tasks using only the keyboard, and listen to a representative page with a screen reader. These steps reveal unlabeled controls, broken focus order, poorly structured headings, contrast failures, and missing alt text—issues that block users but remain invisible to teams who rely on visual cues. Lightweight assessments are fast, inexpensive, and accessible to non-specialists. They also build awareness across teams and provide immediate evidence that accessibility requires coordinated effort.

Identifying Structural Barriers

Structural barriers emerge when templates, navigation, or components behave unpredictably. A navigation menu that requires hovering, a modal that traps keyboard focus, or a carousel that auto-advances without control—all of these create barriers that no amount of content editing can fix. Structural barriers must be addressed at the design-system or engineering layer because they affect every page that uses those components. Identifying these early prevents teams from wasting time fixing symptoms in content while root causes persist in templates.

Creating a Realistic Roadmap

Once you understand your baseline, you want a roadmap that balances ambition with feasibility. Full WCAG 2.2 AA compliance across a legacy site rarely occurs in a single initiative, as templates, CMS components, and content must be updated gradually as other work continues. A realistic roadmap prioritizes changes that improve task completion, reduce legal exposure, and strengthen user confidence. It also phases complex updates across sprints or release cycles. When your roadmap acknowledges real constraints—team capacity, technical debt, upcoming releases—it becomes easier to secure stakeholder alignment and maintain sustainable momentum.

EARLY WINS FOR MOMENTUM

Accessibility maturity grows faster when teams experience early success. You want improvements that are highly visible, easy to deliver, and impactful to users. Early wins build confidence, reduce skepticism, and demonstrate that accessibility enhancements do not require multi-year transformations. They also generate internal support by showing leaders measurable progress in the first month.

Fixing Immediate Barriers

Many accessibility failures are quick to correct. Adding labels to form fields, repairing heading sequences, improving contrast, clarifying link text, and providing alt text for meaningful images all reduce friction for users and strengthen interpretability for machines. These improvements typically require little engineering effort and can be addressed by content teams, designers, or front-end developers. Fixing these issues early not only benefits users immediately but also reduces legal exposure and builds internal momentum.

A Well-Organized Backlog

Accessibility is easier to maintain when all issues flow into a single, well-organized backlog. You want a backlog that distinguishes between template-level, component-level, and page-level issues. This separation helps teams understand which problems require engineering, which need content edits, and which require cross-functional alignment. A structured backlog transforms accessibility from a series of emergencies into a continuous practice supported by predictable workflows. It also makes prioritization clearer because the highest-impact and highest-frequency issues rise naturally to the top.

Establishing Governance Rhythms

Momentum fades without rhythm. You want lightweight rituals—quarterly audits, release checklists, accessibility sign-off for new components, and regular updates to your accessibility statement. These rhythms prevent regressions and keep accessibility aligned with ongoing work rather than isolated as an annual exercise. Governance rhythms also clarify accountability across teams, providing contributors with a shared structure that reinforces consistency over time. When accessibility becomes a habitual part of the workflow, quality improves naturally, and regressions remain rare.

VISIBILITY GAINS

Accessibility improves more than usability; it strengthens the signals that govern search visibility and representation in AI-mediated environments. Clean structure, predictable behavior, and clear relationships all reduce ambiguity for algorithms. When ambiguity drops, confidence rises—and the systems deciding which explanations to surface begin relying on your content more often.

GOVERNANCE AND ORGANIZATIONAL MATURITY

Accessibility fails when teams do not share expectations or when decisions change silently at the edges of the system. You want governance that clearly distributes responsibility, reinforces standards, and prevents regressions from accumulating. Governance does not need to be heavy—it needs to be credible.

Ownership and Accountability

Clear ownership reduces ambiguity. A template owner knows when a component change may introduce a barrier. A content owner knows when labels or headings drift. A product owner knows when features break expected patterns. Accountability transforms accessibility from a special initiative into an everyday quality.

Lightweight Rituals That Prevent Regression

Governance succeeds when it fits naturally into existing rhythms. You want regression checks before each release, small quarterly template audits, and definition-of-done statements that require working keyboard access and predictable focus movement. These rituals catch issues before they become systemic. They also reinforce the idea that accessibility is part of delivering a high-quality experience, not something to retrofit afterward.

TESTING FOR RELIABILITY

Accessibility becomes trustworthy only when tested repeatedly. The most accessible intentions still fail in practice when interactions behave inconsistently, markup changes during redesigns, or new components ignore established patterns.

Automated Checks

Automation quickly catches code-level issues—missing alt attributes, incorrect heading order, invalid ARIA usage, or contrast failures. These checks run at scale and are ideal for preventing regressions during rapid releases.

Manual and Keyboard Testing

Keyboard-only navigation is a mandatory accessibility test.

Every core task must be completable without a mouse, including navigation, form submission, dialogs, and menus. If focus order breaks, focus becomes invisible, or interactions require hover or pointer input, the experience fails—regardless of visual polish. Keyboard failures block users immediately and are among the most common causes of legal complaints. This test should be performed on every major template and after every significant interface change, because no automated tool can reliably detect broken keyboard interaction paths.

Screen Reader and Specialist Testing

Screen readers interpret structure, not appearance. Hearing your own site read aloud reveals mislabeling, missing context, out-of-order headings, and ambiguous relationships. Some issues require specialist input—especially for complex interfaces or highly interactive components—but even limited exposure improves team empathy and structural awareness.

WORKFLOWS THAT PRESERVE ACCESSIBILITY

Your workflows determine whether accessibility improves steadily or degrades quietly. When accessibility is embedded in editorial standards, design processes, engineering models, and release gates, regressions are less likely to slip through.

Editorial Standards

A small set of rules—one H1 per web page, sequential headings, descriptive link text, meaningful alt text—prevents most content-level regressions. When authors internalize these habits, the site becomes easier for users and machines to interpret.

Design-System Defaults

Good defaults eliminate entire categories of accessibility failures. Components with proper roles, visible focus indicators, sufficient contrast, and predictable behavior reduce the need for manual fixes later. Upstream decisions matter more than downstream corrections.

Component Governance

Components drift when teams fork them or modify interactions under pressure. A versioned component library with clear accessibility requirements keeps behavior stable. Stability makes your site easier to interpret and your maintenance more predictable.

Release Gates and Definition of Done

Definition-of-done criteria that require accessible interactions force teams to resolve issues early. By the time the code reaches QA, the structure already supports assistive technologies and machines. Release gates convert accessibility from aspiration into practice.

ACCESSIBILITY AS LEADERSHIP

Accessibility reflects how your organization views its users, its responsibilities, and its long-term credibility. Leaders shape whether accessibility is treated as negotiable or as a standard of quality. When leadership reinforces that accessibility is non-negotiable, teams build workflows that protect it—even under tight deadlines.

Setting Cultural Expectations

Leaders influence whether contributors take accessibility seriously. When expectations drift, accessibility weakens quickly. Leadership sets the tone that accessibility is part of excellence, not a compliance checkbox.

Prioritizing Inclusivity

Inclusive design strengthens reputation and trust. Users who rely on assistive technologies form opinions quickly: predictable interfaces earn loyalty. Accessible experiences demonstrate professionalism and credibility—signals that matter profoundly in competitive markets.

Strengthening Trust and Brand Perception

Accessibility failures are visible failures. Predictable, well-structured, inclusive experiences communicate care and competence. This strengthens your brand in ways that extend far beyond compliance.

BRINGING IT ALL TOGETHER

Accessibility is structural. It influences legal exposure, user satisfaction, search visibility, and how AI systems interpret your meaning. When accessibility improves, clarity improves. When clarity improves, visibility strengthens. The work begins with establishing a baseline, identifying structural barriers, and sequencing early wins. It becomes sustainable through governance, training, and workflows that prevent regressions. Over time, accessibility becomes something the system protects on its own—an operational capability rather than a fragile achievement.

FURTHER READING

- **Book 3—AI Visibility Playbook**—sets policy, standards, and review cycles that keep accessibility reliable.
- **Book 2—Accidental SEO Manager**—offers practical ways to prioritize inclusive work and maintain momentum.

Chapter 13

MULTINATIONAL AND MULTILINGUAL SEO

NAVIGATING GLOBAL SEARCH COMPLEXITY

Expanding into multiple countries and languages introduces constraints that do not exist in single-market SEO. Language, regulation, culture, infrastructure, and user expectations intersect. The challenge is both scale and coordination: how to preserve meaning while allowing content to adapt locally without fragmenting the system that search engines and language models rely on.

International SEO, therefore, becomes an architectural and governance problem before it becomes a tactical one. URL structures, language handling, templates, translation workflows, schema alignment, and release sequencing all determine whether your organization appears coherent or contradictory across markets. When these foundations are governed consistently, visibility scales with relatively low friction. When they are not, even strong local content begins competing with itself.

Market, Language, and Locale Decisions

A language describes how content is written. A region defines legal, commercial, and cultural conditions. A locale combines both. Treating these as interchangeable is one of the most common international SEO failures. An English page written for Canada is not interchangeable with one written for the United States or the United Kingdom, even if the language is shared.

Search engines evaluate regional relevance using both structural signals and content cues. When the wrong locale serves the right language, credibility weakens. Users sense the mismatch immediately, and search systems follow their behavior.

Aligning URL Structures with Expansion Plans

Choosing between ccTLDs, subdomains, and subdirectories is less about theoretical SEO advantage and more about long-term operational discipline. ccTLDs send the strongest geographic signals but multiply maintenance overhead. Subdomains provide separation but fragment authority. Subdirectories consolidate signals but require strict governance.

What matters most is commitment. Organizations that mix structures as they expand create technical debt that becomes difficult to unwind. The right structure is the one your teams can maintain consistently over the years, not the one that looks optimal on a slide.

Regional Search Behavior

Search behavior varies by market in ways that go beyond translation. Financial queries in Germany reflect different decision paths than those in Australia. Travel searches in Japan emphasize certainty and planning detail. Product queries in Brazil often foreground installment pricing.

Even within English-speaking markets, vocabulary and intent diverge meaningfully. Local research and in-market feedback are therefore not optional. Without them, global SEO strategies default to home-market assumptions that underperform elsewhere.

MAKING HREFLANG WORK AT SCALE

The HTML tag hreflang is one of the few signals that explicitly tells search engines which audience a page serves. When it fails, the failure is rarely technical syntax. It is procedural.

International sites break hreflang when URLs change without coordination, when templates drift between markets, or when releases partially deploy across regions. Stability depends on process discipline more than markup correctness.

Canonicals and Hreflang Serve Different Jobs

A canonical tag identifies the preferred version of a page. In most cases, that preferred version is the page itself. A parameterized URL points to its clean counterpart, and variants that represent the same content consolidate into one definitive location. That is the entire purpose of canonicals: to reduce duplication and clarify the core version of a page.

A hreflang cluster is a set of equivalent pages—each in its own language or region—linked horizontally across markets. None of these pages points to another page canonically; each points to itself. A Spanish page is canonical to itself. A French page is canonical to itself. A Canadian English page is canonical to itself. The x-default version, when used, is simply a fallback for users whose language or region does not match any specific variant. It is a routing signal.

Confusion arises only when teams assume these two mechanisms interact. They do not. Canonicals solve duplication. Hreflang solves audience targeting. Keeping this separation clear prevents years of avoidable troubleshooting.

Using x-default Effectively

Some organizations never set an x-default, and that is perfectly acceptable. Others use it to point to a global landing experience: a selector page, a corporate home page, or a route-finding hub that helps users identify the right locale. What matters is intentionality. If x-default points to a specific market, such as the United States, every other region inherits US sentiment by default. That is rarely desirable. A neutral, internationally appropriate page provides far better routing and reduces accidental bias toward one market.

Avoiding Cross-Locale Collisions

Hreflang does not guarantee correct ranking if regional pages are indistinct. This is especially visible among English-language markets. When one version is materially stronger, search engines may elevate it globally despite correct annotations.

The remedy is substantive: regulatory distinctions, localized examples, market-specific offers, vocabulary, and trust signals that demonstrate the page exists for a particular audience.

LOCALIZING FOR MEANING

Localization succeeds when meaning remains stable while expression adapts. Mechanical translation achieves linguistic accuracy but lacks credibility. Users disengage quickly when content feels foreign in tone, examples, or assumptions.

Some content types require strict fidelity—such as definitions, policies, and regulated statements. Others benefit from transcreation, where messaging is reshaped to fit local norms. Knowing which is which is a managerial decision, not a translation one.

Translation versus Transcreation

Certain page types demand strict fidelity to established meaning, including definitions, policy explanations, regulated statements, and eligibility criteria. Other pages benefit from transcreation, which reshapes the message to fit naturally within local communication styles. A product description written for an American audience often sounds too bold for Asian markets, while a Japanese explanation may feel overly formal to Europeans.

In-Market Review as Risk Control

In-market reviewers catch what translation workflows miss: awkward phrasing, misaligned examples, inappropriate tone. Their role is validation. Content that feels native consistently performs better than content that is merely correct.

Maintaining Entity Consistency

Search engines model your brand, products, and services as **entities**. If attributes or definitions vary by language, that model destabilizes. A multilingual glossary that governs product names, attributes, and key terms prevents fragmentation. When concepts change, the glossary changes first.

STRUCTURING SITES FOR LOCAL MARKET BEHAVIOR

Templates that work well in one market often frustrate users in another. Some regions expect dense information early. Others prefer progressive disclosure. These differences affect layout, navigation, and sequencing.

Global templates should therefore provide controlled flexibility. Optional modules allow local adaptation without structural drift. Unconstrained customization produces fragmentation that search engines interpret as inconsistency.

Navigation and Hierarchy

Navigation expresses hierarchy, but hierarchy itself is culturally mediated. Adjusting labels, ordering, or emphasis often delivers more benefit than redesigning navigation entirely. Stability matters more than uniformity.

Regional Requirements

Legal disclosures, pricing rules, warranties, and risk statements vary by region. These must be embedded structurally, not inserted manually. Manual handling guarantees inconsistency over time.

MANAGING GLOBAL TECHNICAL ARCHITECTURE

The strongest international sites maintain a single structural spine while allowing markets to adapt within governed boundaries. Without it, variation multiplies into unpredictability.

URL Pattern Governance

Markets will request exceptions. Some flexibility is reasonable. A controlled naming system—fixed core directories with approved local variants—preserves crawlability while allowing local expression.

Geolocation and Redirects

Geolocation logic is another area where international sites often overcomplicate things. Redirecting users based on IP seems intuitive, but it causes problems when travelers, VPN users, or multi-lingual residents land on your site. More importantly, forced redirects can interfere with crawling and indexing. A best-practice approach is to allow users—and crawlers—to access any market freely, while offering gentle prompts that help people move to their preferred locale.

CDN and Edge Risks

CDNs introduce invisible variability: rewritten URLs, normalized headers, and inconsistent caching. Without centralized governance, two users in the same market may receive different pages. Logging and configuration discipline are essential for diagnosis.

COORDINATING INTERNATIONAL RELEASES

Release failures scale faster internationally. Longer text strings, RTL layouts, and localized components quickly expose template assumptions.

Synchronized launches concentrate risk. Staggered launches surface issues earlier. Either approach works only with disciplined sequencing and communication.

Staggered versus Synchronized Launches

Release failures scale faster internationally. Longer text strings, RTL layouts, and localized components quickly expose template assumptions.

Synchronized launches concentrate risk. Staggered launches surface issues earlier. Either approach works only with disciplined sequencing and communication.

Time Zones and Local Calendars

One of the easiest mistakes a global team can make is scheduling a deployment during a significant holiday in another market. The Lunar New Year in Southeast Asia, or Diwali in India, results in local staff taking up to two weeks of leave. Local teams must be available to validate content, check compliance wording, and verify currency or pricing updates. A release window that looks safe from headquarters may be impossible for in-market teams. Maintaining a shared release calendar, visible to every market, prevents conditions where updates go live with no one available to confirm correctness.

Protecting Language Integrity during Deployments

Language declarations, hreflang links, and locale-specific components must be explicitly checked during releases. Partial rollouts are a common source of contamination across markets.

MULTILINGUAL STRUCTURED DATA

Structured data adds complexity across languages. Attributes vary. Names differ. Units change. Regulatory disclosures diverge.

The underlying entity, however, must remain conceptually stable. A localized schema should reflect the visible reality while mapping back to a unified global model.

Scripts and Encoding

Sites that support languages using multiple scripts—Cyrillic, Kanji, Hangul, Arabic—face additional challenges. They introduce parsing risk. The schema should be generated from shared source data to prevent divergence across templates or markets.

Testing Schema in Multiple Markets

Testing the schema only in the primary market is insufficient. Regional crawling behavior, currency formats, and script handling differ. Testing across markets catches silent failures early.

INTERNATIONAL QA AND MARKET MATURITY

Quality assurance must scale with diversity.

Structural QA

Layout stretch, heading order, component behavior, and semantic consistency must be validated across languages. These checks protect both accessibility and interpretability.

MARKET MATURITY DIFFERENCES

High-maturity markets reward nuance and penalize sloppiness. Emerging markets often reward clarity and structure first. Local search engines introduce additional constraints that require platform-specific expertise.

High-Maturity Markets

In markets like the United States, Japan, Germany, and the UK, search engines have extremely deep signals to work from. Competitors publish optimized content, update frequently, and maintain strong entity consistency. Here, you succeed by refining nuance: improving structured data, tightening content clarity, reinforcing internal linking, and strengthening topical authority. Gains tend to be incremental but durable. Because users expect polished experiences, even minor lapses—such as outdated pricing, slow mobile performance, or unclear navigation—can result in immediate visibility and engagement penalties.

Emerging Markets

Emerging markets often offer disproportionate upside because competition is thinner and user expectations vary more widely. Here, clarity and stability matter more than sophistication. A well-organized site with coherent templates and clear definitions can outperform local players even before you localize fully. However, emerging markets also change quickly, with shifting regulations, new local search platforms, and evolving mobile behaviors. Your approach must be deliberate but flexible, allowing you to adapt faster than local competitors while maintaining global governance.

Markets with Local Search Engines

Some regions rely heavily on search engines other than Google. Examples include Naver in South Korea, Baidu in China, and Seznam in parts of central Europe. These engines interpret signals differently, prioritize different ranking factors, and require different content structures. Optimizing for them often requires local platform expertise and market-specific workflows. A unified global strategy still helps, but you must accept that ranking factors vary and local specialists must shape implementation.

Terminology and Keyword Nuance

Keywords vary dramatically across regions—even within the same language. Australians use "rego" where Americans use "registration." Indians may search for "tuition," while Britons search for "fees." These differences shape search intent and influence your content strategy. Markets with tightly regulated terminology, such as finance or healthcare, also require strict adherence to local phrasing. When you adopt local terminology, you reflect user expectations and signal relevance more strongly than translated keywords ever can.

Cultural Trust Signals

Different markets trust different forms of evidence. Some audiences want detailed specifications and compliance statements. Others rely on expert testimonials, third-party certification, or narrative examples. Understanding which signals resonate in each market helps you create content that feels authoritative locally rather than generically acceptable. If your brand appears foreign in tone or trust cues, users may hesitate—and engagement signals will reflect that hesitation.

GOVERNANCE, MEASUREMENT, AND DRIFT PREVENTION

Without governance, multinational sites fragment. Definitions diverge. Templates fork. Metadata drifts.

Protecting core definitions is non-negotiable. Markets adapt expression, not meaning.

Ownership must exist at the regional level, but within a global framework. Quarterly cross-locale audits surface drift before it becomes systemic.

Measurement must be contextual. Visibility signals differ by market. Cross-market cannibalization is an early warning sign of structural failure.

AI-MEDIATED MULTILINGUAL SEARCH

Generative systems synthesize across languages. Stronger versions of your content influence weaker ones. Structural clarity in one locale can dominate representation globally.

Definitions, lists, and early structure matter disproportionately because models reuse them. When one language version is easier to extract, it becomes the default authority.

Conversational assistants blend content across markets. Without structural harmony, they assemble mismatched explanations that feel incoherent or culturally wrong. Stability across languages is now a visibility requirement, not an optimization.

FUTURE-PROOFING GLOBAL SYSTEMS

Resilient international systems define a minimum standard for launching new markets: adaptable templates, multilingual metadata rules, governed glossaries, schema mappings, and in-market review workflows.

RTL layouts, script variation, and regulatory change must be addressed at the component level. Manual fixes do not scale.

Lifecycle governance matters. Coordinated updates, sunset rules for outdated content, and cross-locale audits prevent slow degradation.

BRINGING IT ALL TOGETHER

Multinational and multilingual SEO succeeds when governance preserves meaning while allowing local expression. Architecture provides the spine. Localization preserves credibility. Structured data reinforces reality. QA and release discipline prevent fragmentation.

Organizations that treat international SEO as a long-term capability—rather than a rollout project—build visibility that endures across markets, languages, and AI-mediated discovery environments.

FURTHER READING

- **Book 2—Accidental SEO Manager**—guides hreflang operations, localization ownership, and cross-market governance.
- **Book 4—Is Our SEO Working?**—helps you interpret locale signals and prevent cross-market cannibalization.

Chapter 14

MANAGING KEYWORDS AND SEARCH INTENT

FROM KEYWORDS TO INTENT GOVERNANCE

Keywords matter only insofar as they reveal what users are trying to accomplish. Modern search systems no longer treat queries as isolated strings of text; they interpret them as signals of intent, context, and decision stage. When planning is anchored solely to keywords, teams optimize language while leaving user uncertainty unresolved. When planning begins with intent, keyword data becomes a diagnostic tool—one that exposes friction, gaps, and misplaced assumptions across the site.

In AI-mediated environments, this distinction becomes critical. Large language models synthesize meaning across pages, not phrases. They reward sites that express tasks and entities consistently, and they struggle with ecosystems that fragment the same intent across multiple, competing explanations. Managing keywords, therefore, is no longer about selecting terms. It is about governing how intent is expressed, reinforced, and maintained across the organization.

ENTITIES AS THE STABLE FRAME

Search engines organize knowledge through entities—concepts that remain stable even as language varies. Users may search for "home loan eligibility," "first-home buyer rules," or "borrowing capacity," but the underlying entity remains the same. Visibility becomes more durable when your content reinforces that entity across the full range of associated tasks rather than chasing individual expressions.

This is why **intent and entities must be grouped together**. Intent explains *why* the user is searching; the entity explains *what the system believes the topic represents*. When those two align, relevance stabilizes. When they diverge, rankings fluctuate, and AI systems hesitate to reuse your explanations.

Smaller or newer brands benefit most from this approach. They may not outrank incumbents on head terms, but they can dominate the surrounding tasks—eligibility checks, comparisons, setup steps, exceptions, and constraints—that shape real decisions. These supporting tasks often carry higher intent and lower ambiguity, making them disproportionately valuable.

INTENT AS A CONTROL MECHANISM

Search intent is a control mechanism. It determines whether a page should exist, what role it plays, and how it should evolve. When intent is defined late—or inferred after drafting—pages tend to accumulate mixed purposes: part explanation, part marketing, part policy reference. These hybrids perform poorly because neither users nor systems can determine what problem they are meant to solve.

At a managerial level, the discipline is simple: **every page must serve a single dominant task**. Secondary questions may be supported, but they must reinforce—not compete with—the primary intent. This constraint does more to prevent drift than any keyword list or optimization tactic.

Industries experience this differently, but the pattern is consistent. Banks lose trust when eligibility rules blur into promotional messaging. Travel brands fail when operational rules are buried inside destination content. Retailers suffer when installation guidance is scattered across product, support, and blog pages. In every case, the failure is caused by intent dilution.

MATCHING PAGE TYPE TO EXPECTATION

Users arrive with expectations shaped by repeated exposure to similar problems. They expect concise definitions, structured comparisons, and procedural guidance that removes ambiguity. When the page type matches the intent, users progress. When it does not, they abandon quickly—and systems learn not to trust the page for that task.

This is an interpretive signal. Search engines and AI systems infer reliability from structural alignment. **A page that behaves like a definition is more likely to be summarized as one. A page that behaves like a checklist is more likely to be reused** in step-based answers. Mismatched structure introduces risk, which reduces reuse.

You influence this outcome by enforcing page roles. Not every query deserves a new page. Often, the correct response is to strengthen an existing page, merge overlapping explanations, or retire material that no longer reflects user behavior. Intent, not demand alone, determines the action.

LANGUAGE GOVERNANCE AND TERMINOLOGY STABILITY

Keyword insights fail when organizations allow multiple labels for the same concept to coexist unchecked. Over time, this produces fragmentation: similar pages using different terms, different formats, and different assumptions about scope. Users notice first. Systems follow.

Governance resolves this by **establishing authoritative definitions**. One page anchors the concept. Other pages support it. Synonyms may appear, but meaning remains unified. This discipline reduces editorial drift and strengthens entity recognition across the site.

The problem is accumulation. Teams update pages independently, using language that makes sense locally, without reviewing adjacent content. Without a shared glossary or definition anchor, divergence becomes inevitable. Stability requires intention, not correction after the fact.

PREVENTING WASTE AND PAGE SPRAWL

Intent governs growth. When keywords rather than tasks justify new pages, ecosystems expand without purpose. Thin content accumulates. Overlapping explanations compete. Maintenance costs rise while clarity declines.

A mature intent model treats keyword clusters as triggers for evaluation, not production. Sometimes the correct response is consolidation. Sometimes it is a deletion. Sometimes it is improving a single authoritative page so it absorbs demand that previously scattered across multiple weak ones.

This restraint is coherence. Lean ecosystems are easier for users to navigate and easier for systems to interpret. Intent keeps the site legible as it evolves.

STRUCTURAL DECISIONS—SPLIT OR COMBINE

Deciding whether to split content across pages or combine it into a single page is a governance decision. Splitting clarifies when users arrive with genuinely distinct tasks or when depth would otherwise obscure meaning. Combining clarifies when multiple pages repeat the same explanation with minor variation.

The wrong choice dilutes intent. Too much splitting will fragment understanding. Too much combining buries essential distinctions. The correct choice preserves a single interpretive center while supporting the natural progression of user questions.

Managers add value here by resisting local optimization. The decision must serve the cluster, not the page owner.

EXECUTIVE-LEVEL INTERPRETATION OF INTENT

Executives do not need keyword artifacts. They need visibility into where users struggle, where confusion affects revenue or risk, and where clarity creates opportunity. Intent analysis provides that lens when it is framed correctly.

Useful reporting surfaces patterns, not terms: recurring eligibility confusion, repeated comparison behavior, persistent troubleshooting demand, or abandoned decision paths. These patterns signal structural issues that product, UX, legal, or operations teams must address. When intent is framed as user evidence, it earns attention beyond marketing.

ALIGNING INTENT WITH ROADMAPS

Intent patterns lose value if they remain inside SEO workflows. Their real impact emerges when they inform roadmaps. Repeated searches for configuration steps, policy clarifications, or exception handling indicate friction within the product or service—not just in the content.

When teams see the same task surface repeatedly, they recognize the cost of ambiguity. Eligibility confusion becomes a compliance risk. Baggage uncertainty becomes a booking loss. Installation confusion becomes a returns problem. Intent turns search data into cross-functional evidence.

STRUCTURE AS REINFORCEMENT

Structure is how intent becomes extractable. Clear openings, predictable subtopics, and consistent depth allow systems to reuse content confidently. This is where entity alignment, E-E-A-T, and AI visibility intersect—not through optimization, but through coherence.

Pages that reinforce meaning structurally earn durable representation: featured explanations, AI summaries, and reference-level reuse. Pages that drift structurally may still rank, but they are reused less often because their meaning costs more to interpret.

CLOSING THE LOOP

Managing keywords today means governing intent over time. It requires resisting fragmentation, enforcing clarity, and treating search behavior as evidence of user struggle rather than as a list of terms to target. When intent guides structure, language, and lifecycle decisions, visibility stabilizes—even as phrasing, platforms, and interfaces evolve.

The organizations that succeed are not those with the largest keyword sets, but those with the clearest understanding of what their users are trying to do—and the discipline to express that understanding consistently.

FURTHER READING

- **Book 2—Accidental SEO Manager**—turns intent research into briefs, ownership, and "definition of done."
- **Book 4—Is Our SEO Working?**—validates whether intent and page purpose are reflected in measurable signals.

Chapter 15

CONTENT QUALITY

WHY QUALITY CARRIES MEANING

Quality is how you make your organization legible. Every page teaches users, search engines, and large language models what you do, what you mean, and what should be trusted. When quality holds, meaning moves cleanly across templates, channels, and interfaces. When it slips, systems infer. Users guess. Models improvise. The cost shows up as misrepresentation, lower reuse in AI outputs, and recurring internal effort spent explaining what the site should have made obvious.

Quality is also a governance signal. A coherent, accurate page does not merely "perform better." It reduces ambiguity across the entire ecosystem, which is the underlying condition modern search depends on.

WHAT QUALITY ENABLES

When a page clearly resolves a concept, people and machines converge on the same interpretation. That convergence is the payoff. It speeds decisions, lowers abandonment, and reduces the "follow-up search" behavior that signals the page failed to complete the task.

You also see the operational side quickly. Clear content reduces escalations to Legal because the boundaries and claims are explicit. It reduces support load because people can self-serve without having to translate vague language into practical meaning. It reduces editorial churn because the first version is structurally sound, not a draft that requires repeated rescue.

WHERE TRUST ORIGINATES

Trust forms when independent evaluators reach the same conclusion without coordination. Users trust you when you stay consistent: the same terms, the same meanings, the same boundaries, the same truth. Search engines trust you when your entity signals remain stable across pages and over time. Large language models trust you when your explanations resolve cleanly under paraphrasing and reuse.

Quality is the set of conditions that lets systems treat your content as low-risk to interpret and reuse.

PROTECTING ANCHOR PAGES

Not all pages carry the same interpretive risk. A handful of pages serve as anchors:

- Category definitions
- Core service explanations
- Primary product models
- Eligibility or policy pages, and
- Regulated disclosures.

These pages shape how everything around them is interpreted.

If an anchor drifts, the error propagates. Search engines reclassify related pages within a distorted frame. Models reuse the wrong definition and then spread it across related questions. You do not need perfection everywhere to reduce risk; you need stability in the places that define meaning for the rest of the site.

QUALITY IS THE ENVIRONMENT YOU CREATE

You do not "own quality" because you edit sentences. You own it because you control the environment that determines whether quality survives contact with reality: who can change definitions, how templates evolve, how cross-team updates are coordinated, and where truth lives when multiple systems publish the same claim.

Most poor-quality outcomes are not craft failures. They are ownership failures. When decision rights are unclear, content becomes a negotiation between teams and time. Drift becomes normal.

HOW SEARCH ENGINES INTERPRET QUALITY

Search engines infer quality through coherence. They model what your pages represent, how concepts relate, and whether your ecosystem behaves consistently. The central question is whether your signals converge.

A page becomes easier to classify when the opening declares purpose, the structure reinforces the topic boundary, and the relationships between ideas are stable across similar pages. When those signals conflict—headings imply one thing, body text implies another, metadata points elsewhere—confidence drops. Rankings fluctuate, indexing becomes less predictable, and the system becomes more conservative about featuring or summarizing you.

Stability is the compounding factor. When your purpose and definitions stay steady, trust accumulates. When meaning shifts frequently, every update forces re-evaluation, and re-evaluation introduces uncertainty. Optimization applied to an unstable base produces volatility rather than durable gains.

HOW LARGE LANGUAGE MODELS EVALUATE QUALITY

Models do not "rank" your page. They decide whether your meaning is safe to reuse. That changes the threshold. Your content must remain coherent when fragmented, quoted partially, paraphrased, and placed alongside competing explanations.

Models treat reliability as resolution. If a concept resolves consistently across contexts, the model treats it as stable. If it resolves differently across pages or sections, the model does not simply choose a winner; it often reduces confidence across the set and looks elsewhere. That is why multiple near-duplicate pages with slight differences can be worse than one imperfect page: you create uncertainty that the model cannot reconcile during synthesis.

Fan-out makes this stricter. When a query expands into sub-questions—definitions, boundaries, prerequisites, exceptions—the model needs anchors that do not wobble. You do not need to anticipate every variation, but you do need to define the truth of your entities clearly enough that the surrounding logic can be built without guessing.

Extractability follows from that. Passages are reused when they stand alone cleanly. When a paragraph mixes explanation, caveats, and implications without resolving the core claim, the model tends to skip it or dilute it. The exclusion is risk management.

WHERE QUALITY BREAKS FIRST

Quality rarely collapses in a single moment. It degrades through small, seemingly harmless decisions that become expensive globally.

One failure mode is page multiplication. A new landing page appears for a campaign. Another team creates a parallel page because they did not know the first existed. Soon, you have multiple pages "defining" the same thing with slight variations. Search engines may treat that as duplication and uncertainty. Models often treat it as a conflict in truth and reduce reuse across all versions.

Another failure mode is silent meaning shifts. Product changes, policy updates, and renamed offerings—then content lags behind reality. The page remains polished, but it is no longer true. Systems detect these mismatches through cross-signals such as feeds, structured data, third-party references, and broader web context. You may not see the failure until visibility softens or AI summaries become inaccurate.

A subtler failure mode is reactive writing. Teams try to "optimize for AI" by adding volume, chasing variations, or adopting generic AI-sounding phrasing. The output may look comprehensive, but it often fails to anchor on stable definitions, relationships, and boundaries. It becomes noise disguised as completeness.

DIAGNOSING QUALITY WITH A MANAGER LENS

A quality diagnosis is a search for patterns that distort meaning and weaken trust.

Start by sampling high-impact clusters rather than attempting to read everything. Look for definitional stability: do multiple pages introduce the same concept in compatible ways? Then look for entity drift: are the same attributes and claims presented consistently across related pages, systems, and markets?

Test extractability briefly. Read a key paragraph and ask whether it would still make sense if quoted alone. If it depends on the surrounding context to clarify what it "really means," it is fragile. Fragile passages are less likely to be reused accurately in AI outputs and more likely to be paraphrased into something you did not intend.

Finally, look beyond the website. If your product pages, support content, feeds, and metadata describe the same thing differently, you do not have a content problem. You have a truth-distribution problem. Fixing that upstream stabilizes quality everywhere downstream.

STRENGTHENING QUALITY AT SCALE

Scaling quality is about reducing the number of ways meaning can diverge.

You gain leverage from a **definition library**: concise, factual anchors for core entities that teams can inherit rather than reinvent. You also gain leverage from structural patterns: consistent ways to open, scope, and sequence information so that similar pages behave consistently. That predictability helps users orient quickly and helps systems classify and reuse your content with less uncertainty.

Variability across teams is inevitable—marketing, product, and support will emphasize different aspects. Your goal is a shared truth and stable boundaries. When teams share the same definitions and relationships, they can vary their tone without fragmenting meaning.

Templates and components matter more than most organizations admit. They convey meaning through repetition. A product card, a comparison module, a services panel—these are not design elements; they are semantic carriers. If components fork or drift, you create multiple representations of the same entity. Stability in shared components is a direct quality-control mechanism.

IDENTIFIABLE EXPERTISE

Quality improves when your content is clearly attributable to people qualified to stand behind it. You do not need celebrity authorship or elaborate profile pages. You need a simple accountability layer that makes expertise legible: who owns the truth, who reviewed it, and when it was last confirmed. This reduces organizational drift because teams stop treating explanations as anonymous copy that can be rewritten casually. It also reduces interpretive risk for search engines and AI systems, which favor sources that appear maintained, traceable, and consistent over time.

Accountability works best when it is operational rather than promotional. A short author or reviewer block that reflects real decision rights—product owner, compliance reviewer, clinical reviewer, lead engineer—signals that the page is maintained by someone with authority to keep it accurate. You can keep this lightweight: name, role, relevant credentials when it matters, and a link to an internal or public profile if it is stable. The goal is to make the source of truth visible.

The largest failure mode is inconsistency. If some high-impact pages show review ownership and others do not, or if bios and revision dates are stale, the accountability layer becomes noise. Treat it like a component: standardized placement, consistent fields, and change control. When accountability is consistent across your reference pages—definitions, policies, safety guidance, documentation—you make quality easier to maintain and harder to dilute.

MANAGING QUALITY DEBT

Quality debt accumulates when unclear pages remain live, outdated claims persist, and overlapping pages compete for the same intent. Left alone, it becomes a drag on every future initiative because each update must navigate a landscape of contradictions.

You reduce quality debt by prioritizing anchors first: the pages and components that define categories, offerings, and high-stakes claims. You do not need a heroic rewrite program. A steady cadence of consolidation, retirement, and anchor reinforcement prevents the debt from compounding.

GOVERNANCE AND DECISION RIGHTS

Quality holds when decision rights are explicit. Someone must own entity definitions. Someone must own the attribute set that represents "what stays true." Someone must own template and component changes that affect meaning across hundreds of pages.

Governance does not need to be heavy. It needs to be credible. A small set of guardrails—a shared glossary, definition anchors, template rules, and a clear escalation path for meaning conflicts—prevents drift more effectively than large committees.

Most quality failures happen during change: migrations, redesigns, navigation shifts, CMS updates, and localization rollouts. If those projects ship without meaning checks, quality degrades invisibly. You protect quality by making "meaning regression" a normal consideration, alongside performance and functionality.

QUALITY AS COMPETITIVE ADVANTAGE

Quality becomes strategic when it produces durable clarity at scale. Clarity differentiates because it is difficult to copy: competitors can mimic messaging, but they cannot easily replicate a coherent meaning system backed by governance, stable templates, and consistent truth distribution.

It also reduces risk. Predictable meaning lowers misclassification, reduces contradictory AI summaries, and prevents the slow erosion that looks like "algorithm volatility" but is often self-inflicted inconsistency.

When your organization's outputs convey stable meaning, every improvement compounds. New pages inherit clarity. New contributors align faster. Systems reuse your explanations more confidently. That is the advantage: not better writing in isolation, but a business that remains interpretable as interfaces evolve.

FURTHER READING

- **Book 3—AI Visibility Playbook**—creates organizational safeguards that prevent low-value patterns at scale.
- **Book 4—Is Our SEO Working?**—operationalizes quality audits and ties improvements to observed outcomes.

Chapter 16

LINK SIGNALS AND AUTHORITY

WHY LINKS STILL MATTER

Links remain one of the few signals that originate entirely outside your organization. Unlike content, metadata, or structure—each of which you control—links reflect independent judgment. When another organization cites your material, it signals that your explanation reduced their risk of being wrong. That external dependency is what makes links durable, even as search systems and AI interfaces evolve.

In an AI-mediated environment, **links matter less as votes and more as evidence of reliance**. Search engines and language models use links to infer which sources the wider ecosystem depends on when accuracy matters. This is why links still influence visibility long after tactical link building has lost relevance. They are not endorsements of popularity; they are indicators of trust in the face of uncertainty.

WHAT AUTHORITY REALLY IS

Authority is a learned pattern. Systems infer authority by observing whether your explanations remain consistent, whether external sources continue to reference them, and whether those references persist even as time, context, and phrasing change.

Authority strengthens when your organization behaves predictably over time. It weakens when meaning drifts. Importantly, authority does not disappear when links are removed; it erodes when **new links stop forming**. That distinction should matter to you because authority loss usually begins internally, long before dashboards reflect decline.

AUTHORITY IN AI-MEDIATED SEARCH

AI systems do not reconcile conflicting explanations. When definitions, examples, or relationships shift across your ecosystem, language models reduce reuse rather than choosing a winner. A page may continue ranking, but its explanations stop appearing in summaries, comparisons, and conversational answers.

In this environment, links act as confirmation that your meaning can be reused without reinterpretation. When external sites continue referencing your explanations verbatim—or close to it—AI systems gain confidence that your material represents a stable understanding of the topic. When those references fade, models infer uncertainty, even if traffic metrics remain unchanged.

HOW AUTHORITY COMPOUNDS

Authority compounds when external references reinforce the same core explanations over time. This typically occurs around a small number of pages that serve as reference points: definitions, policy summaries, rules, specifications, disclosures, or documentation that others depend on to explain something accurately.

When these pages remain structurally stable, links compound naturally. When they change meaning—even subtly—authority resets. The compounding effect is slow, but the loss is abrupt. A single redesign, reworded definition, or restructured table can invalidate years of accumulated trust if it breaks the assumptions external sources relied on when citing you.

WHERE AUTHORITY BREAKS

Authority does not collapse because competitors publish more content. It breaks when your organization introduces inconsistency.

Common failure patterns include:

- redefining a concept without coordinating downstream pages
- restructuring a reference page without preserving its semantic spine
- maintaining parallel explanations that drift over time
- allowing high-trust pages to change casually during redesigns

When this happens, external citations do not disappear immediately. They stop renewing. Over time, systems come to regard your explanations as no longer dependable, and authority dissipates quietly.

LINKS AS SYSTEMIC SIGNALS

Links should be understood as **confirmation signals**, not growth levers. They confirm that your organization has become part of someone else's workflow—journalistic, regulatory, educational, or operational. That role cannot be forced, only maintained.

From a managerial perspective, the key insight is this: links amplify whatever meaning already exists. If meaning is stable, links compound authority. If meaning drifts, links amplify confusion until external trust withdraws.

GOVERNANCE AND AUTHORITY

Authority is governed long before it is measured. Organizations that treat definitions, terminology, and reference pages as shared assets retain authority through change. Those that allow uncoordinated updates lose it unpredictably.

It is an operational outcome of how seriously the organization treats accuracy, consistency, and long-term clarity. Governance does not create authority; without it, authority cannot survive at scale.

INDUSTRY REALITY

Authority takes different forms across industries, but the underlying mechanism remains consistent.

- Banks accumulate authority through stable disclosures and explanations that outlast campaigns.
- Travel brands earn authority through dependable rules and guidance that others reuse under pressure.
- Retailers gain authority when their explanations reduce uncertainty at decision points.
- Software companies build authority when documentation remains reliable across versions.

In every case, authority emerges from **dependability**, not volume.

AUTHORITY AS ADVANTAGE

When authority is strong, visibility becomes resilient. Rankings fluctuate less. AI systems reuse your explanations more confidently. Journalists cite you without hesitation. Customers trust your guidance faster.

This resilience is the strategic advantage. Authority reduces volatility. It lowers the cost of change. It allows the organization to evolve without having to re-earn trust every time something shifts.

YOUR ROLE

Your role is to protect the conditions that sustain authority. That means recognizing which pages the outside world depends on, slowing changes that affect them, and ensuring clarity survives redesigns, restructurings, and handovers. Leave link-seeking to your team.

Authority is preserved through restraint. Organizations that understand this stop chasing signals and start protecting meaning. When meaning holds, authority follows.

SUMMARY—AUTHORITY ENDURES WHEN MEANING HOLDS

Links still matter because they reflect external reliance. Authority grows when your explanations remain dependable across time, context, and reuse. It weakens when meaning drifts, even if metrics lag.

For managers, the lesson is straightforward: treat authority as an asset that must survive change. When you protect the explanations others rely on, links continue to form naturally, AI systems continue to reuse your material, and visibility becomes predictable rather than fragile.

That is the real advantage of authority in the AI era.

FURTHER READING

- **Book 2—Accidental SEO Manager**—focuses on building link-worthy assets and preventing counterproductive requests.
- **Book 4—Is Our SEO Working?**—separates real authority movement from noise using stable indicators.

Chapter 17

COMPETITIVE INTELLIGENCE AND MARKET POSITIONING

Meaning of Competitive Intelligence

Competitive intelligence is about understanding how meaning is established in your market before a user ever reaches your site. By the time someone evaluates your offering, their expectations have already been shaped by competitors, search results, third-party explanations, and prior exposure to how similar problems are usually framed.

Your role is to understand that interpretive environment. You are not competing in isolation. You are competing against the explanations, definitions, and mental models that users have already absorbed. Competitive intelligence gives you visibility into those models so you can position your own content with intent rather than reacting unthinkingly to what others publish.

When this work is done well, positioning becomes clearer, comparisons become easier for users, and the momentum of evaluation shifts in your favor. When ignored, even strong products feel harder to understand than weaker alternatives that communicate more clearly.

WHO YOUR REAL COMPETITORS ARE

Your real competitors are not always the organizations selling similar products. They are the sources that shape how users understand the problem you solve.

Some competitors are obvious: vendors offering comparable solutions to the same audience. Others are indirect but just as influential: documentation hubs, industry blogs, regulatory explainers, comparison engines, and authoritative reference sites. These sources often appear earlier in the journey and establish what "normal," "expected," or "complete" explanations look like.

Users carry those expectations with them. When they arrive at your pages, they are not asking whether your solution is good in absolute terms. They are asking whether it aligns with—or improves upon—the explanations they have already seen.

Competitive intelligence starts by identifying which organizations shape those expectations and how consistently they do so.

HOW COMPETITORS SHAPE USER EXPECTATIONS

Competitors influence user evaluation long before direct comparison begins. They do this through patterns rather than persuasion.

Users absorb:

- how quickly a concept is defined
- how terminology is introduced and reused
- how complexity is staged
- which distinctions are treated as important
- which risks or trade-offs are acknowledged

These patterns form a baseline. When your content aligns with that baseline, users progress smoothly. When it diverges without an apparent reason, users slow down, reread, or return to search results—not because your offering is inferior, but because interpretation requires more effort.

This is why competitive intelligence focuses on *structure and framing*, not claims. You are studying how competitors make understanding feel easy—or difficult.

POSITIONING

Strong positioning does not rely on differentiation statements. It relies on reducing the cognitive work required to understand what you offer relative to alternatives.

In competitive environments, users gravitate toward sources that:

- explain the problem space clearly
- make distinctions explicit
- acknowledge constraints honestly
- maintain stable language across pages

When competitors achieve this, they appear more credible—even if their solution is not objectively stronger. When you achieve it better, you gain an advantage without adding features, pricing incentives, or marketing claims.

Your positioning improves when evaluators can explain your offering to someone else without hesitation. Competitive intelligence helps you identify where that explanation currently falters.

STUDYING COMPETITIVE PATTERNS THAT MATTER

Effective competitive analysis looks for convergence. When multiple competitors explain the same concept in similar ways, they reveal shared expectations in the market.

Pay attention to:

- how core concepts are introduced
- where examples appear

- how edge cases are handled
- what is emphasized early versus deferred

These patterns indicate what users now consider "table stakes" for clarity. Ignoring them does not make your message distinctive; it makes it harder to process.

At the same time, look for divergence—places where competitors gloss over complexity, avoid definition, or compress important distinctions. These gaps often represent your best positioning opportunities.

COMPETITIVE INTELLIGENCE IN SEARCH CONTEXTS

Search environments amplify competitive influence by teaching users what answers should look like.

High-visibility pages—definitions, comparisons, explainers—become reference models. Even when users do not consciously remember the source, they internalize the structure. When your content later deviates, it feels unfamiliar or incomplete.

This effect matters even when search competitors are not commercial. Encyclopedic entries, regulatory summaries, and technical documentation often set the interpretive frame. Your content is judged against those standards whether you intend it or not.

Competitive intelligence, therefore, includes studying which non-vendor pages dominate discovery and what explanatory norms they reinforce.

IDENTIFYING WHERE POSITIONING BREAKS DOWN

Positioning weaknesses rarely appear as obvious failures. They surface as hesitation.

Signs include:

- users comparing repeatedly without progressing
- persistent "versus" searches after exposure
- reliance on third-party explainers to validate understanding
- inconsistent terminology across your own pages

These behaviors indicate that users are doing interpretive work that your content should have resolved. Competitive intelligence helps you trace that friction back to its source—often a missing definition, an unstable term, or an assumption competitors have already trained users to expect.

When you remove that friction, positioning strengthens immediately, even without changing the underlying offering.

USING COMPARISONS WITHOUT UNDERMINING CREDIBILITY

Comparisons are most effective when they help users reason, not when they assert superiority.

Competitors often weaken trust by avoiding trade-offs or oversimplifying adoption complexity. This creates an opening. When you acknowledge constraints, dependencies, or decision criteria explicitly, your explanation feels more grounded and therefore more credible.

The goal is to help evaluators understand why differences matter. This reduces perceived risk and makes your positioning feel more realistic than competitors' slogans or selective framing.

MAINTAINING MEANING STABILITY AS A COMPETITIVE ADVANTAGE

One of the strongest competitive advantages is meaning stability.

When terminology, definitions, and conceptual boundaries remain consistent across pages, users feel oriented. They stop questioning whether they understand the product correctly. This stability compounds across the journey, making evaluation faster and more confident.

Competitors who lack this discipline force users to reconcile contradictions. Even subtle variation creates doubt. Over time, organizations that maintain stable meaning appear more mature and trustworthy, regardless of feature parity.

Competitive intelligence reveals where competitors drift—and where your own language may already be doing the same.

TURNING COMPETITIVE INSIGHT INTO ACTION

Competitive intelligence creates value only when it influences decisions.

The most effective applications are small and targeted:

- refining a definition that users compare repeatedly
- restructuring an explanation to match learned expectations
- clarifying a distinction competitors leave vague
- stabilizing terminology across key pages

These changes rarely require new content. They require alignment. When your teams understand how users are already being taught to think about the problem, they make better decisions without needing constant guidance.

SUSTAINING COMPETITIVE AWARENESS OVER TIME

Competitive positioning is not a one-time exercise. Markets evolve through gradual shifts in language, emphasis, and explanation style.

A lightweight, ongoing review—focused on how competitors frame problems rather than what they launch—keeps you aligned with changing expectations. This prevents sudden repositioning efforts that often introduce confusion instead of clarity.

When competitive intelligence becomes habitual, positioning stabilizes. You adjust incrementally, preserve coherence, and avoid the drift that weakens trust over time.

COMPETITIVE POSITIONING AS ORGANIZATIONAL DISCIPLINE

A single team does not own positioning. Marketing, product, documentation, support, and sales all contribute to how your offering is interpreted.

Competitive intelligence provides the shared context that aligns these groups. When everyone understands the expectations users bring, the organization communicates more coherently—even across formats and touchpoints.

This coherence is what evaluators experience as confidence.

BRINGING IT ALL TOGETHER

Competitive intelligence is about understanding the interpretive environment in which your audience operates and positioning your explanations accordingly.

When you study how competitors shape expectations, you gain leverage. You stop competing on volume or claims and start competing on clarity, stability, and ease of understanding. Over time, this discipline makes your organization easier to evaluate, easier to trust, and harder to displace—even in crowded markets.

Positioning improves not because you say more, but because you remove the work users should never have had to do in the first place.

FURTHER READING

- **Book 2—Accidental SEO Manager**—helps you convert competitive insight into positioning and execution decisions.
- **Book 4—Is Our SEO Working?**—shows how to monitor competitive movement and quantify impact.

Chapter 18

SPAM, QUALITY SIGNALS, AND LOW-VALUE CONTENT RISKS

WHY SPAM RISK IS A MANAGEMENT PROBLEM

Spam is no longer defined by overtly malicious tactics or blatant attempts to manipulate rankings. Modern search and AI systems treat spam risk as a pattern problem: when content consistently creates friction, confusion, or interpretive doubt at scale, systems reduce reliance on it regardless of intent. This means your exposure is not limited to bad actors or questionable SEO practices.

Well-intentioned organizations drift into spam-like profiles through accumulation—outdated pages, overlapping explanations, template expansion, and ungoverned growth that gradually weaken clarity.

Your responsibility is to prevent your content ecosystem from exhibiting behaviors that appear unreliable when evaluated holistically. Spam risk today is an organizational failure mode, not a copywriting error. When systems lose confidence, they do not issue warnings or penalties. They quietly stop reusing, recommending, and elevating your material, causing visibility to erode long before rankings visibly collapse.

HOW SYSTEMS ACTUALLY INFER QUALITY

Search and AI systems do not judge quality by effort, intent, or polish. They infer quality from outcomes. They observe how content behaves when matched to an expected task and compare that behavior against competing explanations. This evaluation is continuous and comparative, not isolated.

Several signals converge in that assessment:

- whether users progress confidently or retreat to search
- whether navigation supports understanding or creates disorientation
- whether explanations resolve uncertainty or multiply it
- whether related pages reinforce meaning or contradict each other

When evaluators hesitate, reformulate queries, or abandon pages in search of clarity elsewhere, systems treat that behavior as evidence of low usefulness. A competitor with a simpler structure and a tighter scope can outperform you without superior products or deeper content. Quality, therefore, emerges at the intersection of user comprehension and ecosystem consistency. Strengthening one almost always improves the other.

LOW-VALUE CONTENT VERSUS SPAM

Low-value content and spam differ in motivation but often converge in effect. Search systems do not infer publisher intent; they model observable outcomes. Pages that feel repetitive, vague, padded, or unresolved interrupt user progress in the same way spam does at scale.

This is where many organizations misjudge their risk. Content created in good faith can still fragment authority, dilute clarity, and introduce uncertainty when multiplied across large ecosystems. Over time, these patterns suppress visibility not because individual pages are "bad," but because the system no longer trusts the environment they sit within. Reducing spam risk, therefore, is not about defending intent. It is about eliminating structural patterns that consistently create friction when your content is consumed at scale.

When Good Content Starts Behaving Like Spam

Even strong pages can inherit spam-like signals when they exist inside weak neighborhoods. Pages surrounded by near-duplicates, filler variants, or doorway-like expansions suffer collateral damage because systems assess clusters rather than URLs in isolation. This is why cleanup efforts focused only on visibly weak pages rarely work. The risk is structural, and it must be addressed at the ecosystem level.

PATTERNS THAT CREATE SPAM RISK

Spam risk emerges through repeatable organizational behaviors rather than isolated decisions. These patterns are rarely visible when reviewing individual pages, but become obvious when clusters are viewed collectively.

Thin Content Expansion

Thin pages appear when coverage grows faster than explanation. Templates multiply, categories expand, and variants proliferate without adding new understanding. Common drivers include splitting minor variations into separate pages, duplicating regional content without meaningful differentiation, or layering campaign pages on top of existing explanations.

Users struggle to identify what actually differs, and systems observe shallow engagement across many URLs instead of strong engagement on one. Over time, this pattern weakens trust and suppresses visibility across the entire topic area.

Redundant and Overlapping Explanations

Redundancy emerges when multiple teams address the same topic independently. Each page may seem reasonable on its own, but together they force evaluators to choose between versions. Systems respond by weakening all of them rather than selecting a winner. Consolidation restores trust by producing a single authoritative explanation that removes ambiguity for both users and machines.

Template-Driven Filler

Templates enable scale, but filler appears when templates dictate content rather than guide it. Repeated introductions, identical section flows, and mandatory disclaimers signal interchangeability. Evaluators quickly sense that the page exists to occupy space rather than resolve a task, and systems detect this through repetition in structure, phrasing, and semantic coverage. Templates should constrain meaning and structure, not manufacture volume.

OVER-OPTIMIZATION AS A TRUST FAILURE

Over-optimization is no longer a ranking trick; it is a credibility problem. Content engineered for capture rather than comprehension creates immediate friction for evaluators and weakens trust signals for systems.

Unnatural Language

Keyword excess produces mechanical prose that users skim or abandon. This usually stems from fragmented ownership rather than bad intent: reviewers preserve phrases "for SEO," templates repeat terms, and edits accumulate without consolidation. The correction is to restore sentence-level purpose, so each paragraph resolves a question rather than restates relevance.

Forced Internal Linking

Links added to meet quotas or reinforce keywords disrupt interpretive flow. When every paragraph contains links that do not advance understanding, navigation becomes noise. Healthy linking supports conceptual progression, resolves likely next questions, and reinforces cluster logic rather than forcing movement.

Overstated Claims

Exaggeration creates interpretive work. When constraints, dependencies, or limits are omitted, evaluators must infer what is missing. Systems mirror this hesitation through unstable engagement signals. Measured confidence outperforms optimism because it reduces doubt at the moment of evaluation.

SYSTEMIC QUALITY DEGRADATION

Quality rarely collapses in one place. It weakens across clusters when new pages are added without revisiting original structures, definitions expand unevenly, examples drift, and depth becomes inconsistent. From a distance, the cluster no longer guides users through a coherent progression of ideas. Systems respond by reducing confidence in the entire topic area rather than penalizing individual pages.

Suppression without Penalty

Most visibility loss is selective neglect. Systems quietly deprioritize areas that consistently produce hesitation or contradiction. This is why spam risk often feels invisible until recovery becomes expensive.

RECOVERING FROM SPAM-LIKE PATTERNS

Recovery follows a deliberate sequence grounded in behavior and structure rather than metrics alone.

Identify High-Risk Zones

Risk concentrates in legacy sections, rapidly expanded categories, deep subtopics rarely reviewed, and clusters with many low-engagement variants. Start where behavior shows confusion rather than where traffic is highest.

Consolidate for Clarity

Consolidation produces immediate gains by removing contradiction, concentrating authority, simplifying maintenance, and restoring a single interpretive anchor. Users do not want to choose between explanations; they want resolution.

Use Behavior to Set Priorities

Behavioral signals—short dwell time, rapid backtracking, repeated reformulations, erratic navigation—indicate where clarity is failing. Improving these pages yields greater visibility gains than polishing already-strong assets.

GOVERNANCE AS SPAM PREVENTION

Governance is the only durable defense against spam-like drift. Without it, improvements decay and weak patterns re-emerge.

Standards That Preserve Meaning

Standards define when new pages are justified, what constitutes sufficient depth, how definitions are introduced, and when consolidation is required. Without shared standards, quality degrades unevenly and invisibly.

Shared Definition of "Helpful"

Quality collapses when teams optimize for local success without shared intent. You prevent conflict by making evaluator comprehension the universal success criterion across roles.

Monitoring Drift over Time

Quarterly cluster-level reviews surface early warning signs. You are checking coherence, not prose.

BUILDING LONG-TERM RESILIENCE

The most effective protection against spam-like signals is an environment that resists degradation as the site grows. Content ecosystems evolve continuously—new products are added, features change, regions expand, and teams publish in parallel.

Without structural guardrails, even well-written content drifts toward fragmentation. Resilience comes from making clarity the default and ambiguity expensive. When definitions are stable, page purposes are explicit, and growth is governed, low-value patterns struggle to take root.

Preventing Regression

Regression occurs when quality improvements are treated as one-off fixes rather than as preserved conditions. A cluster may be cleaned up successfully, only to weaken again when new pages are added under time pressure or when ownership changes. Preventing regression requires defining what must remain stable: core definitions, page purpose boundaries, acceptable depth, and consolidation rules. When teams understand that quality signals are cumulative—and that weak additions can dilute strong assets—they become more deliberate about publishing decisions. Regression slows when contributors work within clear constraints and when editors have the authority to say no to unnecessary expansion.

Product Variation Pages as a Hidden Spam Risk

One of the most common modern sources of thin content comes from product variation pages. These pages are often created for legitimate operational reasons—different models, SKUs, trims, plans, colors, capacities, or configurations—but they frequently add little explanatory value beyond repeating a shared base description. To search systems, large sets of near-identical variation pages resemble known low-quality and doorway patterns, even when created in good faith.

The risk intensifies when:

- variations differ only by minor attributes (color, size, region, plan tier)
- each variation has its own URL with duplicated copy
- differences are implied rather than explained
- users must compare multiple pages to understand what actually changes

From a system perspective, this looks like footprint inflation rather than clarification. Engagement fragments, authority disperses, and evaluators hesitate because meaning is spread thinly across many URLs. A more resilient approach consolidates shared explanations into a canonical base page. It expresses variation through structured components—tables, selectors, or clearly bounded subsections—so differences are explicit without multiplying pages unnecessarily. This preserves clarity, reduces spam-like signals, and concentrates authority where it matters.

Protecting High-Influence Pages

Some pages shape perception far beyond their traffic volume. These include conceptual introductions, comparison explainers, eligibility or rules pages, and mid-journey validation content that evaluators rely on to confirm understanding. When these pages are vague, padded, or fragmented, doubt spreads quickly across the ecosystem. When they are clear, stable, and well-maintained, they anchor trust everywhere else. Protecting these pages means limiting casual edits, preserving structural clarity during redesigns, and ensuring that updates refine meaning rather than reset it. Strengthening a small number of high-influence pages often does more to reduce spam risk than broad, shallow cleanups.

Aligning Quality with Positioning

Quality and positioning reinforce each other. When your positioning is clear—what problem you solve, for whom, and under what conditions—it becomes easier to decide what does *not* need a page. This restraint reduces filler, duplication, and speculative content, thereby strengthening clarity. Conversely, when positioning is vague, teams compensate by publishing more, hoping coverage will substitute for definition. That expansion increases the likelihood of thin pages, overlapping explanations, and spam-like patterns. Aligning quality with positioning turns clarity into a control mechanism: fewer pages, stronger explanations, and a system that search engines and AI models can interpret with confidence.

THE STRATEGIC ROLE OF QUALITY SIGNALS

The risk today is appearing unreliable at scale. Search engines and AI systems reward environments that resolve uncertainty, behave predictably, and evolve without fragmenting meaning. Your leverage lies in deciding when consolidation is better than expansion, when variation should be expressed structurally rather than through new pages, and when clarity is more valuable than coverage. When quality is treated as a cumulative asset—protected through governance rather than repaired through audits—visibility becomes more stable, authority compounds, and spam risk diminishes naturally rather than reactively.

FURTHER READING

- **Book 3—AI Visibility Playbook—**codifies standards that prevent manipulative or thin patterns from creeping in.
- **Book 4—Is Our SEO Working?—**supports early-warning detection and recovery tracking.

Chapter 19

QUALITY ASSURANCE AND VISIBILITY RISK

THE ROLE OF QUALITY ASSURANCE

Quality assurance exists to prevent visibility loss before it becomes measurable. Unlike audits, which diagnose problems after they surface, QA establishes the conditions that keep clarity, consistency, and interpretability stable as content evolves. Its value lies in protecting the system from slow degradation caused by parallel authorship, incremental updates, product changes, and organizational growth.

You should view QA as a structural risk control. It ensures that the explanations your organization depends on—definitions, frameworks, mid-journey guidance, and decision material—continue to behave predictably over time. When QA works, quality does not spike and then decay; it remains durable, even as contributors change and pressure increases.

HOW QUALITY DEGRADES WITHOUT OVERSIGHT

Quality rarely collapses suddenly. It erodes through small, reasonable decisions made in isolation.

Conceptual Drift

Drift appears when the same idea is introduced differently across pages, teams, or update cycles. A definition expands in one place, contracts in another, or shifts emphasis without coordination. Each instance seems harmless, but evaluators encounter inconsistencies and must reconcile their meanings themselves. Over time, trust weakens—not because information is wrong, but because it is unstable.

Coverage Imbalance

Clusters weaken when some pages deepen while adjacent ones remain shallow. Evaluators expect a consistent level of treatment as they move laterally. When depth varies unpredictably, users infer uncertainty about scope or maturity. QA surfaces these imbalances early, before they shape perception.

Legacy Persistence

Older pages often carry disproportionate influence. They rank, they attract links, and they shape first impressions—even when terminology, workflows, or assumptions no longer reflect reality. Without QA, these pages remain authoritative but misleading, quietly undermining newer material.

DEFINING A QUALITY FRAMEWORK THAT HOLDS UNDER PRESSURE

Quality assurance requires explicit expectations. Without them, reviewing becomes subjective and inconsistent.

Making Quality Reviewable

"Good" must translate into observable criteria. This includes how definitions are introduced, how much context a page must provide, how examples are used to resolve uncertainty, and how terminology aligns with existing material. When these criteria are documented, review shifts from opinion to evaluation.

Using Standards as Guardrails

Effective standards limit drift without constraining judgment. They define the minimum depth, the required contextual elements, and the acceptable variation. They do not prescribe tone, but they protect meaning. Guardrails allow teams to move quickly without fragmenting the system.

INTEGRATING QA INTO EVERYDAY WORK

QA only prevents risk when it operates upstream, not as a final checkpoint.

Authoring with Awareness

Quality improves when authors are prompted to reuse existing definitions, check for overlapping material, and understand where a page fits within a larger cluster before drafting. These cues reduce duplication at the moment it forms.

Reviewing for System Impact

Review should extend beyond page correctness. Effective QA asks whether an update introduces conceptual conflict, shifts boundaries, or alters how related pages will be interpreted. This perspective prevents localized improvements from weakening the ecosystem.

MANAGING UPDATES AND CONTENT LIFECYCLES

Every page requires periodic decisions, not indefinite preservation.

Refresh, Rewrite, or Retire

A refresh updates examples or terminology while preserving structure. A rewrite is required when intent or coherence has degraded. Retirement is appropriate when a page duplicates stronger material or no longer aligns with how users search or decide. QA provides the discipline to make these calls without attachment to past effort.

Responding to Product Change

Product evolution introduces acute risk. New capabilities, renamed features, or altered workflows can invalidate large sections of existing content. QA coordination ensures terminology updates propagate consistently and that older explanations do not contradict newer ones.

PREVENTING THIN AND FRAGMENTED CONTENT

One of the most persistent QA risks arises from scale.

Product and Variation Pages

Large catalogs and configurable offerings often generate dozens of near-identical pages—variants, trims, regions, editions. While each page may be legitimate, collectively they can resemble doorway patterns if they do not add distinct explanatory value. QA helps determine when variations should be consolidated, when differences merit dedicated explanation, and when repetition creates interpretive noise that search systems may treat as low quality.

Template Overreach

Pages that follow identical structures regardless of topic signal volume over intent. QA protects against filler by allowing templates to guide, not dictate, structure—removing sections that add no clarity and reinforcing those that do.

USING QA AS A VISIBILITY RISK CONTROL

Quality assurance is a preventive mechanism against suppression, not a reaction to penalties.

Early Risk Signals

High abandonment, repeated query reformulation, lateral bouncing between similar pages, and inconsistent terminology across linked material indicate rising risk. QA processes prioritize intervention based on these signals rather than traffic alone.

Concentrating Authority

Consolidation is one of the most effective QA actions. Merging overlapping explanations into a single authoritative page strengthens clarity, concentrates signals, and simplifies maintenance. QA provides the mandate to do this before duplication becomes systemic.

CROSS-FUNCTIONAL QUALITY OWNERSHIP

Quality cannot be sustained by one team.

Shared Responsibility

Design influences interpretability. Engineering influences access and behavior. Product shapes conceptual truth. Support reveals confusion patterns. QA aligns these perspectives around a shared goal: evaluator comprehension.

Coordinated Review for Complex Topics

Integrations, advanced workflows, and regulatory explanations benefit from multi-team review. This prevents contradictions, clarifies boundaries, and ensures explanations reflect real usage rather than isolated assumptions.

MAKING QUALITY DURABLE

Sustained quality depends on habit, not heroics.

Preventing Regression

Improvements decay unless reinforced. QA embeds expectations into workflows so clarity remains the default. When contributors understand why standards exist, they recognize when decisions introduce risk.

Protecting High-Influence Pages

Some pages shape perception disproportionately: definitions, conceptual introductions, and mid-journey explanations. QA prioritizes these assets because they anchor how evaluators interpret everything else.

QUALITY ASSURANCE AS STRATEGIC INFRASTRUCTURE

Quality assurance is infrastructure. It preserves visibility by preserving meaning, preventing drift, and maintaining coherence as the organization scales. When QA is active, content evolves without fragmentation. When it is absent, even strong material degrades quietly.

Your leverage as a manager lies in making quality repeatable. When clarity is governed rather than inspected, visibility stabilizes, trust compounds, and risk declines—not because teams move more slowly, but because they move together.

FURTHER READING

- **Book 3—AI Visibility Playbook**—defines QA roles, review gates, and escalation paths that hold under pressure.
- **Book 4—Is Our SEO Working?**—ties QA outcomes to diagnostics and regression monitoring.

Chapter 20

TECHNICAL EXECUTION AND REQUEST WORKFLOWS

WHY EXECUTION DECIDES OUTCOMES

You can have a strong visibility strategy and still lose ground if your changes do not ship predictably. Search systems and large language models evaluate what is served in production, not what was approved in a roadmap, documented in a brief, or discussed in a steering meeting. That reality makes technical execution a managerial concern. Your job is to create conditions where the right work can move through engineering with minimal ambiguity, realistic sequencing, and clear accountability. When you do that well, your technical improvements compound. When you do it poorly, visibility work becomes episodic, fragile, and constantly reset by unrelated releases.

WHERE VISIBILITY WORK GETS STUCK

Execution rarely fails because of a single person's mistake. It fails because work enters delivery systems without sufficient clarity for engineers to size, test, and ship it safely. The most common blockers show up in predictable places: hidden dependencies, priority conflicts, legacy constraints, and timing collisions with release cycles.

Dependencies and Hidden Coupling

Most "small" visibility fixes touch more of the system than they appear to at intake. A canonical rule might live in a shared routing layer, a template change might depend on a design system component, and a rendering mismatch might require adjustments across a front-end framework and an edge cache. If you submit a request without acknowledging those couplings, the ticket becomes a discovery exercise, and delivery slows before it starts. Your leverage is to surface likely dependencies early by naming affected page types, templates, components, and services. In Jira, GitHub Issues, or Azure DevOps, you can link related epics or components so estimation reflects the actual shape of the work. You do not need perfect mapping, but you do need enough signal that engineering can see what might fan out.

Priority Conflicts You Cannot Eliminate

Engineering teams are balancing reliability, security, performance, accessibility, and product velocity. Visibility improvements win attention when they are framed as risk reduction and customer impact, not as "SEO asks." If an engineer hears "we need a meta tag update," it sounds optional. If they hear "this template produces inconsistent canonical resolution and is creating index volatility on revenue-driving pages," it sounds like stability work. This is translation. You are aligning your request with the language product owners and engineering managers already use to protect the platform.

Technical Debt That Turns Simple Work into Risk

Technical debt matters to visibility because debt increases variability. It creates templates that behave differently across environments, markup that changes unexpectedly, and front-end patterns that break under load. It also makes regression risk harder to predict. When you tie debt to search-facing consequences—such as structured data extraction failures, inconsistent rendering, or Core Web Vitals (web performance metrics that measure loading speed, interactivity, and visual stability) regressions—you give engineering leaders a reason to prioritize durable fixes rather than repeated patching. In practice, debt work becomes easier to fund when you can show that it reduces incidents and prevents recurring visibility drops.

MAKE REQUESTS ENGINEER-READY

You cannot control engineering capacity, but you can control the quality of what you submit. A strong request reduces interpretation, shortens diagnostic time, and makes testing straightforward. You should treat every request as a small decision package: what is broken, why it matters, what success looks like, and what constraints apply.

Start With the Problem, Not the Fix

Visibility work slows when you prescribe an implementation without clearly describing the problem. Engineering teams then have to reverse-engineer your intent, challenge assumptions, and re-scope the request anyway. You move faster when you describe what you observed and how it affects evaluators. That typically includes where the issue appears, which page types are involved, and what systems might be contributing. When you lead with the problem, engineers can propose solutions that align with the architecture and are less likely to introduce regressions.

Provide Reproduction and Evidence

If you want predictability, you must reduce investigation time. Give engineers reproducible steps and unmistakable evidence. This is where familiar tools help, even for non-engineers, because they create shared ground. Screenshots are useful when paired with precise URLs and conditions. Lightweight checks such as "view-source," curl requests, or structured data test results can clarify whether the issue is server-side output or client-side rendering. You do not need to overwhelm tickets with artifacts, but you do need enough evidence that someone can quickly validate the problem without a long back-and-forth thread.

Define Scope, Constraints, and Acceptance Criteria

Scope clarity prevents midstream stalls. State what is in scope, what is explicitly out of scope, and what constraints matter most. Constraints might include performance budgets, accessibility requirements, legal disclosures, or limitations of a legacy CMS. Then define acceptance criteria in terms of outcomes so QA and engineers can verify completion without debate. Acceptance criteria are not a technical flourish; they are a managerial guardrail that prevents partial delivery and repeated rework. Examples that work well include: canonical tags resolve consistently, structured data validates without errors, rendering parity holds between server and client output, robots directives match policy, and performance does not regress beyond agreed thresholds.

ALIGN WITH DELIVERY RHYTHMS

Visibility work becomes much easier to deliver when it aligns with engineering cycles. Every organization has its own cadence: fortnightly sprints, monthly release trains, continuous deployment, or seasonal freezes. Your goal is to understand when work can be safely accepted, implemented, validated, and shipped.

Plan Around Freeze Windows and Peak Periods

Freeze windows are where good requests go to die. Retailers freeze during major shopping periods, financial services often freeze around reporting cycles, and SaaS teams may freeze around major launches. Submitting high-impact changes during these windows wastes everyone's time and creates unnecessary tension. A manager-level approach is to maintain a simple shared calendar for high-risk periods and to prepare a queue of "ready-to-ship" visibility tasks before freezes begin. This reduces last-minute pressure and increases the likelihood that important fixes land early enough to matter.

Use Low-Risk Windows for High-Risk Work

Some visibility changes carry outsized risk: template-level revisions, routing adjustments, rendering changes in React or Next.js environments, CDN or caching modifications, and wide schema rollouts. These should be scheduled when monitoring capacity is available, and user impact is lower. You do not need to dictate exact timings, but you should show awareness of operational realities. Engineering leaders trust visibility work more when it arrives with an implicit respect for stability and observability.

CLARIFY ROLES AND ACCOUNTABILITY

Cross-functional execution fails most often when ownership is unclear. Visibility touches engineering, product, design, QA, analytics, and sometimes legal or compliance. You can reduce friction dramatically by making accountability explicit, even in a lightweight form. For each change, you want four questions answered early: who approves, who implements, who validates, and who monitors after release. In Jira, GitHub Projects, or Azure DevOps, this can be as simple as assigning a clear owner, adding a QA contact, and documenting the monitoring expectation.

Work With Engineering Managers and Product Owners

Engineering managers decide how risk is managed and how work is sequenced. Product owners decide whether visibility work competes successfully for roadmap space. Your role is to make the trade-offs legible. You do that by linking the request to specific outcomes: reduced indexing volatility, improved template consistency, fewer regressions, faster rendering, or reduced user confusion on high-value journeys. When you consistently show that visibility work protects platform health, the relationship changes. You stop being a requester and become a risk partner.

Bring QA in Early

Quality assurance is essential to making delivery predictable. Visibility regressions often appear only when the device, region, and environment vary. When QA is engaged early, they can shape test scenarios and prevent releases that "work on my machine" but fail for crawlers or users in production. This is where familiar tools can help teams align quickly: Lighthouse CI or WebPageTest for performance baselines, structured data validators for extraction checks, and simple pre-release crawls for template coverage. You should ensure that verification is planned rather than improvised.

MANAGE DEPENDENCIES AS NORMAL WORK

Dependencies are not an exception in modern environments. They are the default. A design system change can affect the output of structured data. An analytics tag update can affect rendering performance. An A/B test framework can change indexability. Treating dependency mapping as everyday work prevents surprises and reduces midstream negotiation.

Map before You Commit

Before you push a request into a sprint or release train, run a quick dependency scan. Identify which components are affected and who owns them. If your organization uses component ownership conventions in Jira or GitHub, use them. If it does not, create a lightweight ownership list for visibility-sensitive surfaces: templates, routing, header tags, schema generation, internal linking modules, and navigation systems. Strive for faster decisions and fewer stalled handoffs.

Sequence Work to Reduce Rework

Even when dependencies are known, teams waste time when the work order is unclear. If design approval affects template changes, secure it early. If QA capacity is limited, negotiate test windows upfront. If there is a risk of performance regression, agree on baselines and thresholds before implementation begins. Sequencing is a form of managerial leverage because it reduces the number of times work needs to be revisited. It also builds trust because engineering teams see that your requests arrive with a plan that respects their workflow.

HANDLE HIGH-RISK CHANGES WITHOUT FREEZING PROGRESS

High-risk visibility work should move more slowly than low-risk work, but it should still move. The managerial pattern that works is staged delivery: break the work into smaller releases with clear validation points. That may mean shipping scaffolding first, then rolling out changes gradually behind a feature flag, and finally expanding once monitoring confirms stability. This approach aligns with how modern teams ship using CI/CD systems such as GitHub Actions, CircleCI, or Azure Pipelines. Your job is to encourage a delivery plan that protects reliability without turning every change into a prolonged project.

Prototype When Uncertainty Is High

If a change involves structured data, rendering behavior, or performance, prototypes can prevent weeks of debate. A limited test in a staging environment, a single template variant, or a controlled rollout can reveal whether the proposed approach behaves as expected. You do not need to design the prototype. You need to ask for one when uncertainty would otherwise push work into endless planning. Prototypes reduce risk by turning assumptions into observable behavior early.

VERIFY IN PRODUCTION, NOT JUST IN REVIEW

A change is complete when production behavior matches intent, and search systems consistently interpret the result. Many visibility failures stem from environment drift: differences in staging and production caching, configuration flags, rendering modes, or resource accessibility. A manager-level execution practice includes a simple post-deploy verification step that confirms the correct signals are being served.

Confirm Search-Facing Output

Verification should include the basics that determine how pages are classified and reused: canonical resolution, robots directives, structured data extraction, rendering parity, and performance stability. You can use Google Search Console and Bing Webmaster Tools to validate indexing and inspection signals. Third-party crawlers can help confirm template consistency across a representative sample. The point is closing the gap between "we shipped" and "systems interpreted it correctly."

Run Regression Checks That Match Risk

Regression checks should reflect the scope of the change. Template-level work deserves broader sampling than a single-page fix. Changes that touch navigation or internal linking deserve pathway validation, not just page validation. Changes that touch performance deserve baseline comparisons, not anecdotal impressions. When you tie regression checks to risk, QA, and engineering, spend time where they protect the organization, not where they are merely traditional.

CLOSE THE LOOP INTO STRATEGY

Execution creates information that should influence your subsequent decisions. Where did the work stall? Which dependencies repeatedly caused delays? Which types of requests created rework? Which environments behave unpredictably? These are not engineering trivia. They are strategic constraints that determine what you can deliver reliably.

Treat Post-Deploy Notes as Operational Intelligence

A short post-deploy note attached to the ticket is often enough: what shipped, what was validated, what surprised the team, and what should be done differently next time. Over time, these notes reveal patterns that let you improve throughput without escalating pressure. They also create credibility. When you can point to a history of well-run delivery, stakeholders trust your judgment when you call something high-risk or time-sensitive.

Socialize Outcomes without Overselling

Engineers and product teams are more willing to support visibility work when they see clear outcomes: fewer regressions, improved performance, stabilized indexing, reduced user confusion, and clearer interpretability. You do not need elaborate dashboards to do this. A concise update on the issue, a brief message in the team channel, or a summary in a planning meeting builds continuity and trust. The objective is to make visibility work feel like part of platform quality, not a separate agenda.

SCALE EXECUTION WITHOUT CREATING BUREAUCRACY

As organizations grow, delivery pathways become more complex. More teams, more systems, and more approvals increase the likelihood of delay. Your response should not involve adding a heavy process. Your response should be to strengthen the few structures that preserve clarity at scale: a consistent intake standard, explicit ownership, risk-based review, and predictable verification.

Build a Repeatable Request Standard

A scalable standard is consistent and straightforward: problem statement, impact, evidence, scope, constraints, acceptance criteria, and monitoring expectations. When every request follows the same structure, engineers can interpret it quickly, product owners can prioritize it fairly, and QA can validate it reliably. This is the core managerial contribution that improves throughput without requiring additional headcount.

Use Automation Selectively

Automation helps when it catches predictable regressions early. Structured data validation, canonical checks, indexability blockers, and baseline performance checks can often be integrated into existing pipelines without significant disruption. The goal is to add a small number of visibility safeguards within the same CI/CD guardrails that teams already trust. When those safeguards are in place, visibility becomes less dependent on heroics and more on routine.

FURTHER READING

- **Book 2—Accidental SEO Manager**—improves intake, scoping, and collaboration with engineering and product.
- **Book 4—Is Our SEO Working?**—verifies whether technical changes improved the signals that matter.

Chapter 21

WORKING WITH AGENCIES AND EXTERNAL PARTNERS

DECIDING WHETHER YOU NEED A PARTNER

You do not hire an agency because SEO is complex. You hire one because something in your environment makes progress slower, riskier, or less predictable than it should be. That distinction matters. Mature internal teams with clear ownership, stable terminology, and strong engineering relationships often outperform external partners simply because they can move faster inside their own constraints. In those environments, agencies add coordination overhead before they add value.

The clearest signal that you do *not* need a partner is when you have achieved SEO fluency. When your team can diagnose visibility issues quickly, trace them to root causes, and move fixes through engineering without repeated explanation, an external partner is unlikely to improve outcomes. They may offer confirmation, but confirmation alone rarely justifies the cost or complexity of engagement.

Where partners become useful is in **leverage**. You benefit from external support when internal teams are stretched thin, when specialized diagnostics exceed in-house depth, or when you need a comparative perspective that cuts across industries and architectures. In those cases, a partner accelerates learning or execution rather than duplicating it. The mistake many organizations make is engaging agencies to compensate for unclear ownership or weak governance. That dependency never ends well.

WHAT EXTERNAL PARTNERS ARE ACTUALLY GOOD AT

Strong agencies contribute in three specific ways: pattern recognition, surge capacity, and specialized diagnostics. They see enough environments to recognize recurring failure modes early. They can absorb high volumes of work during launches, migrations, or crises. And they often have deep tooling or technical expertise that internal teams do not maintain day to day.

What agencies do *not* do well—at least not sustainably—is hold your narrative together. They do not own your terminology, your internal trade-offs, or your long-term positioning. When agencies are allowed to define strategy, language, or governance, fragmentation follows. The most productive relationships are those in which direction remains internal, and agencies are used deliberately as multipliers.

This distinction changes how you brief partners. You are not asking them to "run SEO." You are asking them to investigate specific questions, extend capacity temporarily, or pressure-test assumptions you already own.

WORKING WITH INDEPENDENT CONSULTANTS

Independent consultants are not miniature agencies. Their value lies almost entirely in judgment rather than throughput. In most cases, they advise, diagnose, frame decisions, and challenge assumptions—but do not implement. This distinction is critical because it changes how you should engage, evaluate, and integrate their work.

Consultants are most valuable when the problem stems from uncertainty. You use them when internal teams disagree, when trade-offs are unclear, or when existing narratives no longer explain observed behavior. Their role is to clarify direction, not to carry work forward. When you ask consultants to implement by default, you often dilute their strongest contribution.

Because consultants are rarely embedded in delivery workflows, their recommendations must be translated internally. This is a design constraint. Their output should inform prioritization, governance, or architectural decisions, not bypass them.

When Consultants Create the Most Value

Independent consultants tend to outperform agencies in specific situations:

- when you need a neutral perspective across internal teams
- when existing frameworks no longer explain performance or risk
- when leadership requires confidence in a decision rather than execution speed
- when governance, terminology, or positioning need to be reset
- when you want pressure-testing, not reinforcement

In these contexts, clarity is the bottleneck. Consultants create leverage by reducing ambiguity early, before execution pathways are chosen.

Avoiding Consultant Failure Modes

Consultants fail differently from agencies. The most common risks include:

- producing abstract models with no delivery path
- diagnosing problems without prioritization
- repeating known theory without situational specificity
- disengaging before internal alignment is achieved

You reduce these risks by insisting that consultant output explicitly supports internal decision-making. Every recommendation should answer at least one of the following:

- What decision does this change?
- What trade-off does this clarify?

- What risk does this reduce?
- What assumption does this invalidate?

If consultant insight does not materially influence a real decision, it is informational rather than strategic.

Consultants and Agencies Are Not Interchangeable

Agencies extend your execution capacity. Consultants extend your thinking capacity.

Agencies integrate into workflows. Consultants inform them.

Agencies are evaluated on delivery. Consultants are assessed on whether decisions improve after they leave.

Treating these roles as interchangeable weakens both.

DEFINING SCOPE BEFORE WORK BEGINS

Most agency failures originate in vague scope, not poor execution. When boundaries are unclear, agencies either overreach—introducing frameworks and language that conflict with your own—or underdeliver by staying safely generic.

Scope must be explicit in three dimensions: strategic authority, operational responsibility, and deliverable format.

Strategic authority always remains internal. Decisions about terminology, positioning, governance, and long-term priorities cannot be outsourced without eroding meaning stability. Agencies may advise, but final decisions must be anchored within the organization.

Operational responsibility *can* be externalized, but only when ownership is clear. Technical audits, structured data validation, JavaScript rendering analysis, performance diagnostics, content reviews, or competitive mapping all work well as agency responsibilities when inputs and outputs are defined tightly.

Deliverables are where many engagements quietly fail. If an agency delivers recommendations that require translation before they can enter your workflows, friction is guaranteed. Deliverables should arrive already shaped for your intake systems, your terminology, and your decision cadence. If you cannot paste an output directly into Jira, Notion, or your review process, you have not defined the format clearly enough.

HOW TO WORK WITH AGENCIES WITHOUT SLOWING YOURSELF DOWN

Agency work succeeds or fails on rhythm. Without predictable communication patterns, context decays quickly. Partners work from outdated assumptions, and recommendations drift away from operational reality.

You do not need frequent meetings, but you do need a stable cadence. A regular check-in exists to preserve shared context, not to generate updates. Its purpose is to keep partners aligned with current priorities, constraints, and delivery windows so work lands in a usable state, not theoretical.

Context sharing is your responsibility. Agencies cannot infer roadmap shifts, internal dependencies, or political constraints unless you make them visible. When partners lack context, their recommendations may be technically sound but operationally unusable. Transparency here is efficiency.

Internal stakeholders must also remain involved. Product owners, engineers, designers, analysts, and QA teams determine whether recommendations can be implemented. When agencies operate in isolation, their work accumulates as reports rather than change. Involving internal stakeholders early prevents rework and keeps agency output grounded.

AVOIDING THE MOST COMMON FAILURE MODES

Agency engagements break down in predictable ways.

The first is treating agencies as order-takers. When partners are reduced to executing isolated requests, their output loses prioritization and coherence. Findings arrive detached from implementation reality, forcing internal teams to interpret and reassemble them later.

The second is fragmenting requests. Disconnected tickets prevent agencies from seeing patterns across systems or content. Each task may be correct in isolation, but collectively they fail to move the needle. Agencies add the most value when they can see the system, not just the symptom.

The third is allowing deliverables to drift into generic templates. When expectations are not explicit, agencies default to safe, reusable formats. These artifacts feel polished but rarely drive decisions. The responsibility for preventing this drift sits with you. Agencies rise to the clarity you enforce.

KNOWING WHEN A PARTNERSHIP SHOULD END

The most important agency decision you will make is when to disengage.

Partnerships should end when internal capability has matured to the point where external input no longer changes decisions. They should also end when deliverables repeatedly fail to integrate into workflows, when recommendations remain surface-level, or when dependency begins replacing internal reasoning.

Ending a partnership cleanly requires preparation. Ensure knowledge has been transferred, documentation consolidated, and ownership clarified. Avoid abrupt exits that strand work mid-stream. A well-managed transition protects continuity and prevents regression.

Firing an agency is not a failure. Prolonging a misaligned relationship is.

Ending Consultant Engagements Deliberately

Independent consultants should usually be disengaged differently from agencies. In many cases, termination is the expected outcome.

Consultant engagements are complete when clarity has been achieved, decisions have been made, and internal teams are aligned enough to proceed without external framing. Prolonging a consultant relationship beyond this point often reduces value, encourages abstraction rather than execution, and delays the transfer of ownership back to internal teams.

You should consider ending a consultant engagement when:

- the core questions they were hired to resolve are answered
- their recommendations have been absorbed into internal plans or governance
- discussions begin repeating rather than advancing decisions
- execution, not diagnosis, becomes the primary constraint

A clean exit is a sign of a successful consulting engagement, not a failed one. Strong consultants expect this and design their work to leave you more capable, not dependent.

Unlike agencies, consultants are often best disengaged once direction is clear, even if implementation has not yet begun.

USING PARTNERS TO BUILD INTERNAL STRENGTH

The healthiest agency relationships reduce dependency over time. Encourage partners to explain their reasoning, not just their conclusions. Ask them to surface diagnostic methods, not just outputs.

Use teach-back moments to ensure internal understanding has genuinely increased.

Internal teams should always retain ownership of measurement, interpretation, and prioritization. Agencies may contribute insight, but your organization must remain the authority on what performance signals mean. When interpretation lives externally, resilience disappears.

As teams mature, work naturally moves in-house. Pattern recognition, routine diagnostics, and smaller investigations should become internal capabilities. Agencies remain valuable for specialized or high-volume work, but strategic fluency must stay internal.

MANAGING MULTIPLE PARTNERS WITHOUT FRAGMENTATION

Multiple partners increase expertise and risk simultaneously. Each agency brings its own terminology, templates, and assumptions, which means fragments quickly.

You prevent this by maintaining a single internal source of truth for definitions, narrative models, and standards. Every partner must work from it. You also need clear domain boundaries so partners complement rather than duplicate each other.

When necessary, facilitate cross-agency alignment directly. Partners rarely coordinate unless you design for it. Even lightweight synchronization prevents conflicting recommendations and reinforces coherence.

ACCOUNTABILITY, CONTRACTS, AND OUTCOMES

Contracts should reinforce clarity, not paperwork. Define success in terms of reduced visibility risk, improved interpretability, fewer regressions, or strengthened delivery—not artifacts produced.

Scope should evolve as your organization evolves. Please review it periodically, adjusting responsibilities as internal capability grows or priorities shift. When performance slips, address it quickly with evidence, not frustration. If it does not improve, disengage decisively.

Strong partnerships are accountable on both sides.

KEEPING DIRECTION INTERNAL

Agencies are force multipliers, not owners. Strategy, terminology, governance, and prioritization must remain anchored inside the organization because they depend on institutional knowledge and cross-functional trust.

External partners amplify your strengths when direction is clear. They undermine coherence when it is not. The discipline lies in managing ownership.

When that ownership is clear, partnerships become accelerators rather than dependencies, and external expertise strengthens your system instead of reshaping it.

FURTHER READING

- **Book 2—Accidental SEO Manager**—sets expectations, defines success, and keeps direction internal.
- **Book 3—AI Visibility Playbook**—maintains standards when work is distributed across multiple vendors.

Chapter 22

SEARCH CONSOLE AND DIAGNOSTIC TOOLS

THE MANAGERIAL ROLE OF DIAGNOSTICS

Why Diagnostics Exist

Diagnostic platforms exist to reduce uncertainty, not to replace judgment. As a manager, you do not use Google Search Console, crawlers, or performance dashboards to chase individual warnings or optimize isolated pages. You use them to understand how search systems interpret your organization at scale and to detect when structural assumptions no longer hold. Diagnostics sit between execution and strategy: they translate system behavior into signals you can use to prioritize risk, guide investment, and maintain stability across change.

At a managerial level, diagnostic tools serve three purposes. They surface early warning signals before visibility loss becomes measurable. They reveal patterns that indicate governance or architectural weaknesses rather than one-off defects. And they provide shared evidence that allows cross-functional teams to align on what matters most. When used correctly, diagnostics help you decide where to intervene and where restraint is the better choice.

What Diagnostics Actually Reveal

Search Console and related platforms show how search systems crawl, render, index, and classify your content. They expose gaps between what teams believe they shipped and what external systems actually perceive. These gaps often appear first as subtle anomalies: partial indexing across a content cluster, inconsistent canonical selection, unstable crawl behavior, or recurring warnings tied to specific templates.

Individually, these signals are rarely decisive. Collectively, they describe whether your visibility system behaves predictably. A stable environment produces consistent patterns over time. An unstable one produces noise, reversals, and unexplained variation. Your role is to watch for persistence and correlation rather than isolated alerts. One warning may be incidental; the same warning recurring across releases or template families usually signals a deeper issue.

INTERPRETING DIAGNOSTIC SIGNALS

Signals That Matter at the Leadership Level

Not every diagnostic signal deserves managerial attention. Leaders should focus on signals that indicate systemic risk or opportunity. These include recurring exclusion patterns across related pages, sudden changes in crawl behavior following deployments, instability in rendering or performance across device classes, and repeated structured data warnings tied to the same content families. These signals suggest that something fundamental—templates, workflows, ownership, or assumptions—has drifted.

Equally important are signals that confirm stability. Consistent indexing across new content, predictable crawl rates after releases, and steady performance metrics indicate that governance is holding. Recognizing stability matters because it prevents unnecessary intervention. Diagnostics are as valuable for telling you when not to act as when escalation is warranted.

Interpreting Diagnostics in Context

Diagnostic data has no meaning in isolation. A rendering delay on a low-impact support page does not carry the same weight as the same delay on a revenue-critical comparison page. An indexing anomaly during a major algorithm rollout may reflect external volatility rather than internal regression. Context determines significance.

Effective interpretation requires triangulating diagnostics with evaluator behavior, competitive movement, and organizational change. If diagnostics show stability but impressions decline, competitive shifts or changing expectations are more likely causes than technical failure. If diagnostics show instability immediately after a release, internal change is the probable driver. This framing prevents teams from misclassifying symptoms and chasing the wrong fixes.

Avoiding Tool-Led Decision-Making

Diagnostic platforms provide signals, not direction. Organizations that allow tools to dictate priorities often oscillate between fixes without addressing root causes. This occurs when teams respond to every warning as if it were equally urgent or when success is defined by clearing dashboards rather than improving system resilience.

As a manager, you set the rule that tools inform investigation, not strategy. The presence of a warning prompts questions rather than immediate action. What pattern does this belong to? Has it appeared before? Is it isolated or clustered? What decision does it affect? This discipline protects teams from reactive cycles and preserves focus on changes that create lasting value.

DIAGNOSTICS AS RISK AND GOVERNANCE INPUTS

Using Diagnostics to Govern Technical Risk

Diagnostics are most effective when treated as indicators of technical risk rather than as checklists. Repeated warnings around the same templates, recurring crawl anomalies after deployments, or chronic performance instability usually reflect fragile architecture or accumulated technical debt. These patterns justify structural investment such as template consolidation, framework modernization, or clearer interface contracts between systems.

By contrast, sporadic, low-impact warnings rarely justify major intervention. Your role is to distinguish between noise and risk and to allocate engineering attention accordingly. Diagnostics provide the evidence needed to make these calls credibly with technical leaders and executives.

Diagnostics and Publishing Discipline

Many diagnostic issues originate upstream in publishing workflows rather than in search systems. Missing metadata, inconsistent headings, or incomplete structured data often reflect unclear ownership, insufficient validation, or fragmented processes. Diagnostic platforms surface these issues because search systems are intolerant of ambiguity at scale.

Managers use diagnostics to pinpoint where workflows break down. If the same issues recur in new content, the problem lies in the process design. Addressing it requires changes to templates, training, or validation gates rather than repeated cleanup work. Diagnostics shift conversations from blame toward system improvement.

Combining Multiple Diagnostic Perspectives

No single tool provides a complete view. Google Search Console only shows how Google interprets your site. Other search engines have their own control panels for site managers. Crawlers reveal structural behavior independent of ranking. Performance dashboards surface user-facing instabilities. Competitive tools provide external context. The value lies in synthesis.

At a managerial level, synthesis means assessing alignment or divergence across signals. When multiple tools point to the same pattern, confidence increases. When they diverge, interpretation becomes critical. Stable diagnostics paired with declining impressions usually indicate competitive pressure. Unstable diagnostics paired with stable outcomes suggest contained risk. Your role is to guide teams toward these interpretations rather than allowing any single tool to dominate decisions.

OPERATING DIAGNOSTICS AS A MANAGEMENT SYSTEM

Establishing Diagnostic Routines

Diagnostics generate value only when reviewed consistently. Reactive use—checking tools only after traffic drops—turns diagnostics into post-mortems. Proactive use turns them into early warning systems. Effective organizations establish lightweight, predictable review rhythms that make deviations visible before they affect evaluators.

Cadence should reflect risk rather than habit. High-impact templates and critical content clusters warrant more frequent review than peripheral areas. What matters is consistency and ownership. Someone must be accountable for noticing patterns and escalating when thresholds are crossed. Without ownership, diagnostics degrade into background noise.

From Signals to Decisions

Diagnostics matter only if they influence decisions. At a managerial level, those decisions typically fall into three categories: whether to pause or proceed with change, where to invest for structural improvement, and when to accept risk. Diagnostic patterns provide evidence for each.

Persistent instability may justify delaying a release. Recurring warnings may support a business case for refactoring. Stable diagnostics during a downturn may justify holding course rather than reacting. When diagnostics are framed this way, they become tools for governance rather than operational distraction.

DIAGNOSTICS IN LONG-TERM STRATEGY

Diagnostics as Strategic Input

Over time, diagnostic patterns reveal more than immediate issues. They show which parts of the ecosystem are fragile, which workflows introduce variability, and which investments produce durable stability. Managers who track these patterns use them to inform longer-term roadmaps, such as consolidating templates, modernizing platforms, clarifying ownership, or simplifying content models.

In this role, diagnostics support strategy rather than interrupt it. They help you choose improvements that reduce future operational burden rather than accumulate short-term fixes. This is where diagnostic maturity separates reactive organizations from resilient ones.

Leading with Diagnostic Literacy

You do not need to operate diagnostic tools to lead effectively, but you do need diagnostic literacy. Literacy allows you to ask better questions, recognize meaningful patterns, and challenge assumptions when teams propose fixes that do not address root causes. It also allows you to communicate visibility risk in terms that executives understand: stability, predictability, and resilience.

When diagnostics are positioned as a shared language rather than a specialist function, they strengthen alignment across engineering, product, content, and leadership. Used this way, they support the central goal of modern SEO management: maintaining clarity and stability in systems that continuously interpret your organization at scale.

FURTHER READING

- **Book 4—Is Our SEO Working?**—deepens diagnostic routines and interpretation beyond tool screenshots.

- **Book 2—Accidental SEO Manager**—helps you communicate
findings and drive the right follow-up work.

Chapter 23

MEASUREMENT AND REPORTING FRAMEWORKS

MEASUREMENT AT MANAGEMENT LEVEL

Measurement as Decision Infrastructure

Measurement exists to support decisions, not to prove activity. At a management level, reporting frameworks provide decision infrastructure: they help leaders understand whether the visibility system is performing as expected, where risk is accumulating, and which interventions warrant attention. This shifts measurement away from performance narration and toward operational confidence. When reporting works well, it reduces uncertainty and shortens decision cycles rather than expanding debate.

Your responsibility is to constrain interpretation. A strong framework limits what can be argued by establishing which signals matter, how they relate to one another, and how movement should be interpreted. This protects teams from reacting to noise and helps executives focus on directional outcomes rather than metric trivia.

What Measurement Is Not

Measurement frameworks are not dashboards filled with metrics, nor are they retrospective scorecards. They are not substitutes for diagnostics, and they do not exist to justify past work. When reporting drifts into explanation-by-volume or metric accumulation, it loses authority. Managers should treat reporting as a controlled abstraction of system behavior, deliberately incomplete yet directionally reliable.

DEFINING THE SIGNAL SET

Selecting Signals That Explain Behavior

Effective reporting begins by choosing a small number of signals that explain how the system behaves. Should these signals consistently answer three questions: Is the system stable? Are evaluators progressing as expected? Is the external context influencing outcomes? Signals that do not help answer one of these questions introduce distraction.

The discipline lies in exclusion. Metrics that fluctuate frequently but lack interpretive value should be removed, even if they appear impressive. A reporting framework gains credibility when stakeholders learn that changes are meaningful, because most numbers don't move most of the time.

Structural, Behavioral, and Context Signals

A mature framework separates signals into three explanatory domains. Structural signals describe whether templates, indexing, rendering, and internal linking behave consistently. Behavioral signals describe whether evaluators can understand, navigate, and progress through your content without friction. Context signals describe forces outside the system, such as seasonality, competitor movement, or platform reinterpretation.

This separation matters because it prevents false attribution. Declines accompanied by structural instability require different action than declines occurring under stable structural conditions. Reporting should make these distinctions explicit rather than leaving teams to infer them.

DESIGNING REPORTING LAYERS

Why Layering Is Non-Negotiable

No single report can serve all audiences. Executives, operational leaders, and specialists require different levels of abstraction. A reporting framework that ignores this reality forces audiences to interpret information not intended for them, increasing misalignment and friction.

Layered reporting ensures that each audience receives information appropriate to its decision authority. Executives see direction and risk. Operational leaders see where attention is required. Specialists see supporting detail when investigation is necessary. The structure of reporting becomes a governance tool in its own right.

Executive-Level Reporting

Executive reporting should remain sparse and interpretive. It exists to answer four questions reliably: What moved, why it moved, whether the movement matters, and what decision or posture is recommended. Executives do not need metric definitions or diagnostic detail; they need confidence that interpretation is grounded and consistent.

A stable executive report builds trust over time because leaders learn how to read it. When structure changes frequently, or new metrics are introduced without necessity, interpretation resets, and confidence erodes. Stability of format is more important than novelty of insight.

Operational and Specialist Views

Operational reporting supports prioritization. It identifies the areas that require attention without prescribing solutions. Specialist views exist to validate hypotheses, not to drive routine decision-making. They should be accessed deliberately rather than pushed by default.

A clear separation between these layers prevents accidental escalation. Teams investigate when needed, but leaders are not pulled into diagnostic depth unless decisions require it.

COMPOSITE INDICATORS AND ABSTRACTION

Why Composite Indicators Matter

Composite indicators translate multiple related signals into a single interpretive construct. They allow managers to discuss structural stability or evaluator clarity without enumerating every contributing metric. This abstraction reduces cognitive load and improves consistency of interpretation across audiences.

Well-designed composites move infrequently and visibly. When they change, stakeholders understand that something meaningful has shifted. This makes reporting calmer and more authoritative, particularly during volatile periods.

Guardrails for Composite Design

Composite indicators must remain transparent and stable. Stakeholders should understand what they represent, even if they do not see every underlying metric. Frequent recalibration undermines trust and invites debate about construction rather than behavior.

Composites should not be optimized for presentation aesthetics. Their purpose is interpretive clarity, not visual appeal. If a composite cannot be explained in a sentence, it is too complex.

INTERPRETING MOVEMENT RESPONSIBLY

Explaining Change without Overreach

Movement only becomes useful when it is explained proportionally. Most visibility changes reflect normal system behavior rather than failure or success. Reporting frameworks should normalize this reality by distinguishing between expected variation and meaningful deviation.

Responsible interpretation avoids absolute claims. It frames explanations as likelihoods supported by evidence and acknowledges uncertainty where appropriate. This builds credibility and prevents reactive decision-making.

Handling Ambiguity in Reporting

Ambiguity is an honest reflection of complex systems. When reporting cannot conclusively explain movement, that uncertainty should be communicated clearly, along with the next steps. Executives value transparency more than false precision.

A framework that allows ambiguity to be stated explicitly is more trusted than one that forces confident explanations for every fluctuation.

TURNING REPORTS INTO DECISIONS

Connecting Insight to Action

Reporting has value only when it informs action. At a management level, this means helping teams decide whether to proceed, pause, invest, or monitor. Reports should therefore conclude with an explicit posture recommendation, even when that recommendation is to maintain course.

This does not mean prescribing tactical fixes. It means clarifying decision direction and sequencing so teams can align effort without confusion.

Prioritization through Explanation

When reporting explains why movement occurred, prioritization becomes rational rather than political. Structural issues justify foundational investment. Behavioral issues justify refining content or the experience. Context-driven movement often justifies patience rather than intervention.

Clear explanation protects teams from mismatched effort and helps executives support decisions with confidence.

MAINTAINING FRAMEWORK STABILITY

Why Stability Outweighs Precision

A reporting framework must remain stable over long periods to be useful. Frequent changes to metrics, composites, or structure reset interpretation and undermine comparability. Precision can be improved incrementally; stability must be preserved deliberately.

Managers should resist the urge to continuously refine frameworks. Change should occur only when the underlying system changes materially or when interpretation consistently fails.

Detecting Drift through Reporting

One of the most important functions of reporting is early detection of drift. Gradual degradation in structural stability, evaluator progression, or clarity often appears in reports before it becomes visible externally. A stable framework makes these weak signals detectable.

By surfacing drift early, reporting supports preventive action rather than reactive recovery.

THE STRATEGIC ROLE OF REPORTING

Reporting as Organizational Memory

Over time, reporting frameworks become a record of how the system behaves across changes, launches, and external shifts. This institutional memory prevents teams from repeating mistakes and helps new leaders quickly understand historical context.

When reporting is treated as a durable asset rather than a disposable artifact, it strengthens governance and continuity.

Elevating Measurement Beyond Metrics

At its most mature, measurement and reporting elevate visibility management from performance tracking to strategic guidance. They allow leaders to see patterns, allocate attention wisely, and maintain confidence in complex environments.

When reporting frameworks are clear, stable, and interpretive, they reinforce the central managerial task of SEO leadership: guiding the system with clarity rather than reacting to its noise.

FURTHER READING

- **Book 4—Is Our SEO Working?**—builds layered reporting, composite indicators, and clear narratives.
- **Book 2—Accidental SEO Manager**—equips you to socialize insights and prioritize work from measurement.

Chapter 24

EXECUTIVE DASHBOARDS AND C-SUITE COMMUNICATION

THE EXECUTIVE DASHBOARD AS A DECISION INTERFACE

Purpose of an Executive Dashboard

An executive dashboard is a decision interface. Its purpose is to help senior leaders decide where to allocate attention, where to intervene, and where to hold course. Unlike operational reporting, which supports diagnosis and improvement, executive dashboards support trade-offs under time pressure. They answer a narrow set of questions:

- Is the system stable?
- Where is risk accumulating?
- What opportunities are emerging?
- What decisions require leadership involvement?

This distinction matters because executives do not consume dashboards passively. They use them to justify prioritization, approve investments, challenge assumptions, and set organizational direction. A dashboard that fails to support these actions invites misinterpretation, overreaction, or disengagement. A well-designed dashboard constrains debate by making the decision context explicit.

What the Dashboard Deliberately Excludes

Executive dashboards gain authority through omission. They do not attempt to represent the full complexity of visibility systems, nor do they surface metrics that require specialist interpretation. Granular diagnostics, vendor-specific indicators, and volatile tactical metrics belong elsewhere. By excluding these, the dashboard protects executive attention and prevents escalation driven by noise rather than risk.

DESIGNING FOR EXECUTIVE CONSUMPTION

Abstraction without Ambiguity

Executives require abstraction, but not vagueness. A dashboard must compress complexity into a small number of interpretable indicators while preserving directional meaning. Composite indicators, trend markers, and clear status framing allow leaders to understand movement without having to interrogate mechanics. Each element should be explainable in a sentence and defensible under scrutiny.

Abstraction fails when indicators cannot be tied back to recognizable system behavior. If leaders cannot understand what an indicator represents, they will either ignore it or attempt to deconstruct it inappropriately. The dashboard should invite questions about decisions, not about metric construction.

Direction, Not Point Values

Executive attention is oriented toward trajectory. Dashboards should emphasize movement over time rather than point-in-time values. Directional signals—improving, stable, drifting, or volatile—help leaders calibrate response. This framing prevents overreaction to normal fluctuation and ensures that intervention is reserved for meaningful change.

Where thresholds are used, they should signal significance rather than perfection. Reports should show whether conditions are deteriorating, recovering, or holding steady.

THE EXECUTIVE NARRATIVE LAYER

Structuring the Conversation

Dashboards do not speak for themselves. Their value emerges in the narrative that accompanies them. Effective executive communication follows a consistent structure: what moved, why it moved, how significant the movement is, and the recommended decision or posture. This structure disciplines discussion and keeps meetings focused on outcomes rather than speculation.

The narrative should be concise and repeatable. Executives benefit from familiarity; when they know how information will be framed, they spend less time orienting and more time deciding.

Framing Risk and Opportunity

Executive dashboards should present both risk and opportunity in proportional terms. Persistent instability, accumulating drift, or weakening evaluator clarity represent risk. Sustained improvements, emerging demand, or competitive openings represent opportunity. Presenting both reinforces credibility and positions visibility as a strategic contributor rather than a defensive function.

Crucially, risk framing should distinguish between controllable and uncontrollable forces. Leaders make better decisions when they understand what the organization can influence and what it must accommodate.

GOVERNING THE DASHBOARD

Ownership and Change Control

An executive dashboard requires clear ownership. Someone must be accountable for its structure, interpretation, and evolution. Without ownership, dashboards degrade as metrics are added ad hoc, definitions shift, and confidence erodes. Change control should be explicit: indicators change only when the system changes or when interpretation consistently fails.

This governance protects the dashboard from metric-shopping and political influence. Executives should trust that what they see is stable, intentional, and aligned with long-term objectives.

Preventing Metric Capture

Executive dashboards are vulnerable to capture by vendor narratives, departmental agendas, or short-term incentives. Guarding against this requires discipline in signal selection and a willingness to resist popular but misleading metrics. The dashboard must reflect organizational reality, not external pressure or internal advocacy.

When leaders challenge indicators, the response should be explanation, not accommodation. Adjusting the dashboard to address discomfort undermines its role as a decision-support tool.

USING DASHBOARDS IN EXECUTIVE FORUMS

Embedding in Leadership Routines

Dashboards create value only when embedded in executive routines. Monthly business reviews, quarterly planning cycles, governance committees, and major release checkpoints are natural forums. Consistent cadence allows leaders to develop intuition about the system and recognize meaningful deviation.

Ad hoc escalation should be the exception. When dashboards surface issues predictably, leaders are less likely to intervene impulsively between cycles.

The Pre-Read and the Meeting

Effective C-suite communication separates consumption from discussion. Dashboards should be distributed as pre-reads, so executives can absorb the information before convening. Meetings then focus on interpretation, trade-offs, and decisions rather than orientation.

This separation reduces performative reporting and encourages substantive dialogue. It also protects teams from being put on the defensive during live interpretation of complex material.

MANAGING EXECUTIVE FAILURE MODES

Preventing Traffic Panic and False Confidence

Executives often fixate on top-line outcomes. When traffic dips, panic ensues; when it rises, underlying risk may be ignored. Dashboards counter this by anchoring discussion in system health rather than outcomes alone. Stable systems with declining exposure require different action than unstable systems with growing traffic.

Your role is to redirect attention from symptoms to the conditions they reflect. This reframing prevents whiplash decisions that damage long-term stability.

Handling Misinterpretation and Escalation

Even well-designed dashboards can be misread. When this happens, correction must be calm and principled. Reiterate the interpretation model, explain why a signal does or does not warrant action, and connect the discussion back to the agreed decision criteria. Consistency over time builds executive discipline and reduces recurrence.

DASHBOARDS AS STRATEGIC INSTRUMENTS

Linking Visibility to Leadership Decisions

Executive dashboards should make the consequences of leadership decisions visible. Choices about staffing, release timing, architectural investment, or market expansion all influence the signals leaders see. When dashboards reflect these relationships, executives develop accountability for long-term health rather than treating visibility as an external outcome.

This linkage elevates dashboards from monitoring tools to strategic instruments. They become part of how leadership evaluates its own effectiveness.

Supporting Long-Term Confidence

Over time, a stable executive dashboard becomes a shared reference point. It allows leaders to see patterns across quarters and years, compare initiatives objectively, and maintain confidence during periods of uncertainty. This continuity is more valuable than precision. It enables governance to function amid change.

THE COMMUNICATION MANDATE

From Reporting to Leadership

The effectiveness of executive dashboards ultimately depends on how they are communicated. Your role is to lead interpretation. You translate system behavior into organizational meaning and guide leaders toward proportionate action.

When dashboards are designed with intent, governed with discipline, and communicated with clarity, they strengthen executive judgment and protect long-term visibility. That is their purpose—and the reason they deserve focused, deliberate attention.

FURTHER READING

- *Book 5—The C-Suite Blind Spot*—aligns dashboards, risk framing, and leadership expectations.

- **Book 4—*Is Our SEO Working?*** —connects dashboard signals to reliable interpretation and action.

Chapter 25

ATTRIBUTION, ROI MODELING, AND BUDGETING

WHY ORGANIC VALUE RESISTS SIMPLE ACCOUNTING

Executives are accustomed to channels that behave transactionally. Spend produces clicks, clicks produce conversions, and the relationship between cost and return can be expressed cleanly in a spreadsheet. Organic visibility does not behave this way, and attempting to force it into the same accounting logic consistently understates its value.

Organic visibility operates upstream and across time. It influences how evaluators understand a problem, which options they consider credible, how confident they feel navigating a decision, and how efficiently they convert once intent crystallizes. Much of this influence occurs before analytics systems record anything meaningful, and much of it is misclassified when it finally appears. The result is more of a category error than a measurement failure: organic value is distributed, cumulative, and indirect by design.

Be sure to reframe the conversation so that value is assessed in terms executives already respect—risk reduction, efficiency gains, and durable commercial advantage.

ATTRIBUTION AS A LEADERSHIP PROBLEM, NOT A TECHNICAL ONE

Attribution breaks down the moment evaluators move across sessions, devices, channels, and time horizons. Organic journeys rarely begin and end in a single visit, and they rarely follow clean channel boundaries. Session-based attribution models compress these journeys into artificial snapshots that favor the last observable touch and erase most of the influence that shaped intent.

This limitation cannot be solved by choosing a better attribution model. First-click, last-click, linear, or algorithmic attribution all fail for the same reason: they attempt to assign ownership to inherently cumulative behavior. Executives do not need to be convinced that attribution tools are flawed; they need to understand what those tools can and cannot represent.

The productive shift is away from credit assignment and toward behavioral impact. Instead of asking which channel "caused" a conversion, you focus on how organic visibility changes evaluator behavior over time. Do evaluators progress with less hesitation? Do they return more frequently? Do they arrive at decision points with stronger intent? These questions align far more closely with how organic value actually manifests.

MAKING INVISIBLE VALUE LEGIBLE

Organic visibility creates value in ways that are rarely visible in isolation. Evaluators who encounter clear, trustworthy explanations often return directly later. They convert through paid channels more efficiently. They require fewer interactions to reach a decision. None of this appears cleanly in organic reports, yet all of it affects revenue.

Executives respond best when this invisible value is framed in terms of observable patterns rather than speculative claims. When

improvements in structural consistency coincide with smoother
evaluator progression, reduced abandonment, or higher downstream
conversion efficiency, those correlations are meaningful even without
direct attribution. Over time, aligning visibility improvements with
commercial outcomes builds credibility.

This is where pattern-based reasoning becomes essential. You are not
presenting proof in the mathematical sense; you are presenting
evidence in the managerial sense. Consistent patterns, supported by
plausible causality and reinforced across multiple cycles, are sufficient
to justify investment.

A PRACTICAL MODEL OF ORGANIC ROI

Organic ROI should be modeled as a capability return rather than a
campaign return. Instead of asking how much revenue a specific
optimization produced, you model how investment strengthens the
system that produces revenue reliably over time.

A useful executive model breaks organic value into three components:

Value creation reflects how visibility expands reach and improves
evaluator engagement. This includes stronger coverage of high-intent
scenarios, clearer explanations in complex journeys, and improved
discovery across the ecosystem.

Value protection reflects the revenue preserved by preventing drift.
Structural inconsistency, degraded templates, and unclear narratives
erode trust long before traffic drops. Preventing that erosion avoids
losses that analytics rarely surface until recovery is expensive.

Value acceleration reflects how organic clarity improves the efficiency
of other channels. Evaluators who arrive informed convert more
readily, reducing acquisition costs and improving return across paid,
email, and direct pathways.

This model resonates with executives because it mirrors how they already think about investment: growth, risk management, and efficiency.

WHY PRECISION MATTERS LESS THAN DIRECTION

Attempts to present organic ROI with false precision can undermine trust. Executives do not expect exact figures when systems are complex and data is incomplete; they expect directional clarity. A credible ROI model explains the relationship between investment and outcome, the time horizon involved, and the risks of underinvestment.

Directional modeling allows you to show how changes in funding affect system strength. Sustained investment improves stability and compounds returns. Reduced investment increases drift, slows progress, and raises the long-term cost of recovery. These relationships are more important to decision-making than a single calculated ROI percentage.

BUDGETING FOR A LIVING SYSTEM

Organic visibility cannot be funded episodically. The ecosystem evolves continuously: evaluator expectations shift, competitors adapt, templates age, and governance must respond. Budgeting, therefore, needs to distinguish between maintaining system health and pursuing new opportunities.

A mature budget framework typically includes three layers.

Core capability funding covers the work required to keep the system stable: governance, diagnostics, template maintenance, performance oversight, and content operations. This funding protects existing value and prevents compounding loss. Treating it as optional invites drift and volatility.

Strategic initiative funding supports deliberate expansion or improvement. This includes new content domains, architectural modernization, scenario refinement, or structural enhancements tied to business growth. These investments are where visibility aligns most clearly with strategy.

Efficiency funding focuses on reducing long-term cost and friction. Template consolidation, workflow simplification, and automation improve velocity and resilience even when they do not produce immediate growth.

Presenting budgets in this way aligns visibility investment with how executives already allocate capital across the organization.

FRAMING ROI AND BUDGET IN EXECUTIVE TERMS

Budget discussions succeed when they are framed around outcomes executives care about: stability, predictability, competitive position, and efficiency. Visibility investment should be positioned as a means to reduce uncertainty and protect revenue, not as a discretionary marketing expense.

Executives also need clarity on time horizons. Organic returns accumulate slowly but persist longer than transactional gains. Turning investment on and off produces volatility, not savings. Making this dynamic explicit helps leaders avoid short-term cuts that create long-term costs.

Scenarios are particularly effective in these conversations. Showing what happens under sustained investment, partial investment, or underfunding makes trade-offs tangible. It also highlights the cost of inaction, which is often more persuasive than projected upside.

PREVENTING BUDGET EROSION

Visibility budgets erode when leaders mistake stability for completion. When performance appears steady, maintenance funding is often questioned. Your role is to show that stability is the outcome of continuous effort, not a signal that effort can stop.

Drift is rarely sudden. It accumulates quietly through small inconsistencies, deferred maintenance, and fragmented ownership. Once confidence erodes, recovery requires far more investment than prevention. Framing maintenance as risk control rather than upkeep helps executives understand its necessity.

Embedding visibility considerations into planning cycles further protects budgets. When visibility is present at the start of the roadmap and investment discussions, it becomes part of the organization's planning rather than a downstream cost.

LINKING INVESTMENT TO LEADERSHIP DECISIONS

Executives are more likely to support organic investment when they see how their own decisions influence outcomes. Staffing levels, release cadence, architectural choices, and prioritization all affect the signals used to judge visibility health.

When ROI discussions make these relationships explicit, visibility becomes a shared responsibility rather than a specialist concern. Leaders see that underinvestment creates risk they ultimately own, and that sustained investment strengthens resilience across the business.

THE EXECUTIVE STANDARD FOR ROI

At the executive level, the standard for ROI is whether investment decisions are defensible, consistent, and aligned with long-term objectives. A strong organic ROI narrative meets that standard by explaining how value is created, protected, and accelerated over time.

When you present organic visibility this way, it stops competing with paid channels on the wrong terms. Instead, it is evaluated as what it actually is: a foundational capability that shapes demand, reduces cost, and stabilizes growth in environments where short-term measurement will always be incomplete.

FURTHER READING

- **Book 4—Is Our SEO Working?**—clarifies attribution pitfalls and builds credible ROI narratives.
- **Book 2 — Accidental SEO Manager** — equips you to link investment to stability, efficiency, and outcomes.
- **Book 5 — The C-Suite Blind Spot** — helps you frame trade-offs and funding decisions for senior leaders.

Chapter 26

VISIBILITY OPERATIONS: THE ENTERPRISE MODEL

THE ENTERPRISE VISIBILITY OPERATING MODEL

At enterprise scale, visibility cannot be managed as a specialist function embedded inside marketing or treated as a distributed responsibility that "everyone owns." It requires an explicit operating model. That model exists to ensure that hundreds of decisions made across product, engineering, content, design, analytics, legal, and external vendors result in a coherent, predictable visibility outcome rather than cumulative drift.

The purpose of an enterprise visibility operating model is coordination. You are not attempting to centralize execution or slow delivery. You are defining how a complex organization makes structural decisions safely, consistently, and at speed. Without an operating model, visibility becomes an emergent property of organizational chaos: sometimes strong, often fragile, and rarely explainable.

At this level, visibility operations serve as a governance layer that sits alongside product operations, engineering operations, and data operations. Its role is to protect structural coherence, evaluator clarity, and system reliability across an ecosystem that no single team fully owns. This is what distinguishes enterprise visibility from scaled SEO. The former is an operating discipline; the latter is an execution function.

THE VISIBILITY OPERATIONS FUNCTION

Enterprises do not need a larger SEO team. They need a Visibility Operations function with clearly defined responsibilities and authority. This function is accountable for how the visibility ecosystem behaves as a system, not for individual rankings, pages, or campaigns.

Visibility Operations owns structural standards, decision sequencing, risk classification, and escalation paths. It defines what "good" looks like for templates, components, instrumentation, and narrative structure, and ensures those definitions are applied consistently across teams and markets. It does not write content, ship code, or design interfaces. Instead, it ensures that those activities align with agreed structural patterns before they scale.

This function also acts as the interpreter between executive intent and operational reality. When leadership sets priorities around growth, efficiency, expansion, or risk reduction, Visibility Operations translates those priorities into guardrails that teams can execute against without constant supervision. When something breaks, Visibility Operations determines whether the issue is local, systemic, or organizational—and routes response accordingly.

DECISION RIGHTS AND ACCOUNTABILITY AT SCALE

Enterprise visibility fails most often because decision rights are implicit rather than explicit. Multiple teams influence templates, rendering, instrumentation, and narrative structure, but no one is clearly accountable for the resulting system behavior. An enterprise model requires a visible, agreed decision-rights map.

Enterprise Visibility Operations Framework

Visibility Operations defines and maintains a RACI-style framework that clarifies responsibility across functions because visibility outcomes emerge from **interdependent decisions**, not isolated execution. Without explicit decision rights, organizations default to informal negotiation, duplicated authority, or silent gaps where no one feels accountable for systemic behavior.

In this framework, **Visibility Operations is accountable for structural coherence and risk**, not for execution. It does not approve copy, ship code, or design interfaces. Instead, it owns the *decision logic* that determines when visibility risk exists, which changes require coordination, and how conflicts are resolved when priorities collide.

Product is **responsible** for defining evaluator scenarios, prioritizing journeys, and sequencing changes based on business intent. Product does not decide how those scenarios are structurally expressed across templates or markets; that responsibility is shared through governed patterns rather than ad hoc design choices.

Engineering is **responsible** for implementation quality, system stability, and adherence to shared components and rendering standards. Engineering is **consulted** on structural decisions that introduce technical risk and is **accountable** for ensuring that approved patterns behave predictably in production environments.

Design is **responsible** for component behavior, layout systems, and interaction patterns, but is **consulted** rather than authoritative on structural sequencing or narrative hierarchy. This prevents visual innovation from inadvertently fragmenting interpretive structure.

Content teams are **responsible** for narrative clarity, definitions, and explanatory flow within approved structural patterns. They are **consulted** on how changes affect evaluator comprehension, but they do not unilaterally redefine template logic or introduce new structural variants.

Analytics is **responsible** for measurement integrity and instrumentation quality and is **consulted** on how structural changes affect signal reliability. Visibility Operations relies on analytics input to determine whether proposed changes increase or reduce interpretive confidence at the system level.

Legal and compliance functions are **consulted** when regulatory or disclosure requirements affect structure or content, but they are not the default owners of template behavior. Their constraints are incorporated into patterns rather than handled as one-off exceptions wherever possible.

Visibility Operations is **accountable** for the coherence of the whole. When signals conflict, when teams disagree, or when a change introduces cross-functional risk, Visibility Operations arbitrates based on system impact rather than local optimization. It determines whether a decision is routine, structural, or critical, and routes it through the appropriate review path.

The practical outcome of this framework is speed with safety. Teams move faster because they know where authority sits. Reviews become lighter because expectations are explicit. Regressions decline because responsibility is structural rather than personal. Most importantly, executives gain confidence that visibility outcomes reflect a governed system—not a collection of well-intentioned but disconnected decisions.

Outcome of the Framework

This framework does not remove autonomy. It removes ambiguity. Teams can move quickly because they know which decisions require consultation, which require review, and which can proceed independently. When accountability is clear, regressions decline not because people are more careful, but because fewer decisions fall through organizational cracks.

Example RACI Table

Decision Domain	Visibility Operations	Product	Engineering	Design	Content	Analytics	Legal / Compliance
Visibility operating standards	**A**	C	C	C	C	C	I
Template structure & hierarchy	**A**	C	R	C	C	I	I
Component behavior & rendering patterns	**A**	I	**R**	C	I	I	I
Evaluator scenarios & journey intent	C	**R**	I	I	C	I	I
Narrative logic & definitions	C	I	I	C	**R**	I	I
Instrumentation standards & KPIs	**A**	I	C	I	I	**R**	I
Change classification (routine / structural/critical)	**A**	C	C	C	C	C	I
Release gating for high-risk templates	**A**	C	**R**	C	C	C	I
Incident response & root-cause framing	**A**	I	**R**	I	I	C	I
Portfolio prioritization (what to standardize, isolate, retire)	**A**	C	C	C	C	C	I

Decision Domain	Visibility Operations	Product	Engineering	Design	Content	Analytics	Legal / Compliance
Vendor & platform governance	**A**	I	C	C	I	C	C
Regulatory structural constraints	C	I	I	I	C	I	**R**

Bolded entries indicate primary accountability or execution ownership.

Legend:

- **R** = Responsible (does the work)
- **A** = Accountable (owns the outcome)
- **C** = Consulted (provides input)
- **I** = Informed (kept aware)

CHANGE CLASSIFICATION AS AN OPERATING PRIMITIVE

Not all changes are equal. Treating every change the same is one of the fastest ways for enterprises to create unnecessary friction or miss real risks. Visibility Operations introduces a formal change classification model that governs review depth and sequencing.

Routine changes follow established patterns and do not alter structural logic. These move quickly with minimal oversight. Structural changes affect templates, components, narrative sequencing, metadata logic, or instrumentation models. These require cross-functional review because their impact cascades across large sections of the ecosystem. Critical changes affect high-risk templates, core journeys, global components, or shared infrastructure. These require explicit gating, validation, and rollback planning.

This classification model becomes a shared language. Teams no longer debate whether a change "needs review" based on opinion or politics. The class of change determines the process automatically. This reduces friction while increasing safety, which is the core trade-off enterprise operations must manage.

RELEASE GATING FOR HIGH-RISK TEMPLATES

Enterprise ecosystems include templates whose failures carry disproportionate risk: category pages, product hubs, onboarding flows, documentation roots, and region-wide landing structures. These assets require release gating, not because teams are untrustworthy, but because the cost of failure is asymmetrical.

Visibility Operations defines release conditions for these templates. Structural integrity must be validated. Rendering behavior must be consistent across devices and environments. Instrumentation must conform to canonical definitions. Narrative logic must match established patterns. If these conditions are not met, the release does not proceed.

Gating is not bureaucracy when it is predictable. Teams accept gates when they are known in advance, applied consistently, and focused on system behavior rather than subjective quality judgments. Over time, gating reduces incidents because teams design changes to pass gates rather than treating review as an afterthought.

MANAGING THE ENTERPRISE VISIBILITY PORTFOLIO

Enterprises do not manage a website. They manage a portfolio of assets with varying levels of risk, value, and operational complexity. Visibility Operations treats this ecosystem as a portfolio rather than a flat surface.

That portfolio includes template families and component libraries, markets and regions, products and evaluator journeys, platforms and technology stacks, and vendors and external dependencies. Each dimension concentrates risk differently. Some templates create outsized impact. Some regions drift faster. Some platforms behave inconsistently. Some vendors bypass internal standards.

Portfolio management allows prioritization. Visibility Operations identifies where standardization creates leverage, where isolation reduces risk, where variation is justified, and where retirement is overdue. This prevents the common enterprise failure of attempting to standardize everything while effectively governing nothing.

ENTERPRISE FAILURE MODES

Certain failure patterns recur across large organizations, regardless of industry. Recognizing them early is a core function of Visibility Operations.

One failure mode is unchecked template proliferation. Teams create new variants to solve local problems, but there is no retirement path. Over time, the organization maintains dozens of near-identical templates, each drifting slightly, each increasing cognitive and operational load.

Another is divergent instrumentation. Different business units measure similar behavior differently, leading to conflicting KPIs and irreconcilable dashboards. Executives lose trust because reports disagree, not because data is wrong, but because standards never converged.

Experiment platforms introduce another failure mode. When experimentation tools inject structural variance directly into production without component constraints, they quietly undermine consistency. Tests conclude, but their side effects remain.

Regional narrative drift is equally common. Local teams adapt definitions and explanations independently until the same concept means different things in different markets. Evaluators notice long before dashboards do.

Finally, vendor tooling often bypasses internal standards. Third-party widgets, plug-ins, and scripts introduce behavior no one fully owns. Without governance, external dependencies become structural liabilities.

COORDINATING DISTRIBUTED TEAMS

Visibility Operations does not force teams into identical workflows. It gives them a shared interpretive lens. When teams understand how their decisions affect system behavior, coordination improves without a heavy process.

Shared principles—clarity over novelty, structure before variation, predictability before personalization—guide decisions when documentation is incomplete or timelines compress. Cross-functional rituals reinforce these principles, creating predictable forums where alignment occurs before drift sets in.

Coordination succeeds when teams stop negotiating preferences and start stewarding a shared system.

MANAGING ARCHITECTURAL AND VENDOR COMPLEXITY

Enterprise stacks are heterogeneous by default. Legacy systems, parallel platforms, regional deployments, and vendor integrations coexist. Visibility Operations does not attempt to simplify architecture wholesale. It prevents architectural diversity from producing behavioral inconsistency.

This includes containing legacy systems, standardizing shared components, governing vendor defaults, and maintaining a register of external dependencies with explicit ownership. When third-party tools do not conform to standards, they are deliberately isolated or phased out rather than tolerated indefinitely.

MEASURING OPERATING MATURITY

An enterprise operating model must be measurable. Visibility Operations tracks maturity through behaviors, not vanity metrics. Template coherence, rendering stability, instrumentation consistency, incident response discipline, review predictability, regional alignment, and decision velocity provide a reliable picture of system fitness.

These dimensions are assessed through evidence, not sentiment. Did the last structural change follow the classification model? Did the last incident produce a reusable pattern update? Are regional templates converging or diverging?

Maturity measurement aligns teams around improvement rather than blame.

SUSTAINING THE ENTERPRISE MODEL

Enterprise visibility is sustained through organizational memory. Patterns, standards, and decisions must live in structures rather than individuals. Component libraries, documented rationales, predictable rituals, and stable dashboards ensure continuity through turnover, growth, and transformation.

The most mature organizations distinguish clearly between where originality belongs and where it does not. Innovation belongs in problem framing and evaluator empathy. Structural consistency belongs in templates, components, and instrumentation. When that distinction holds, enterprises scale without fragmentation.

Visibility Operations exists to make that possible.

FURTHER READING

- **Book 3 — AI Visibility Playbook** — supports enterprise guardrails, component standards, and vendor governance.
- **Book 2 — Accidental SEO Manager** — reinforces leadership of distributed contributors and operating rhythms.

Chapter 27

PROCESS FRAMEWORKS AND WORKFLOW CHECKPOINTS

SEO AS AN OPERATIONAL SYSTEM

In large organizations, visibility does not fail because teams lack expertise. It fails because decisions move through the organization without a shared process that protects structure, meaning, and sequence. SEO at scale is therefore not a set of tactics or reviews; it is an operational system that governs how work enters, progresses, ships, and learns.

From a managerial standpoint, the objective is simple: ensure that decisions affecting visibility behave predictably regardless of which team makes them. This chapter defines the minimum process framework required to achieve that outcome. It does not add a new governance theory. It translates the enterprise operating model into day-to-day execution.

THE ENTERPRISE SEO PROCESS LIFECYCLE

A durable SEO process follows a small number of repeatable phases. Each phase exists to prevent a specific class of failure. When any phase is skipped or weakened, regressions become likely.

The lifecycle is a control system.

Intake Alignment

All SEO failures are easier to prevent before work begins than to fix later. Intake alignment ensures that work enters the system with sufficient clarity to proceed safely.

At intake, teams must be able to answer four questions clearly:

- What evaluator scenario does this work support?
- Which template or component family does it affect?
- Does it introduce structural change or reuse existing patterns?
- Does it alter meaning, sequencing, or interpretation?

This step is about preventing ambiguous work from consuming sprint capacity and creating downstream rework.

Design and Narrative Alignment

Meaning is shaped before code is written. Design and narrative alignment are the points where structural logic and explanatory flow are validated together.

At this stage, SEO evaluates whether the proposed layout, hierarchy, and content flow reinforce established patterns or introduce new interpretive behavior. The question is whether evaluators will interpret the page consistently with the rest of the ecosystem.

If a change alters structural logic, it is reclassified as structural work and routed accordingly.

Implementation Alignment

Implementation alignment confirms that approved patterns survive translation into production behavior.

This checkpoint does not involve line-by-line review. It validates outcomes: predictable rendering, stable linking behavior, correct canonical intent, and consistency with the agreed template family. The goal is to ensure that local implementation choices have not quietly altered system behavior.

Pre-Release Validation

Pre-release validation exists to stop high-impact regressions from reaching users.

Before launch, SEO confirms that the work behaves as expected across devices and environments and that it does not introduce unintended variation. This is where release gating applies for high-risk templates, not as a judgment call, but as a defined operating rule.

If validation fails, the release pauses.

Post-Release Learning

Once live, the system must verify that reality matches intent.

Post-release learning compares expected behavior with observed patterns: evaluator progression, engagement anomalies, structural stability, and early signals of drift. The objective is institutional learning.

When learning loops are consistent, the organization stops repeating the same mistakes. When they are skipped, regressions recur, and confidence erodes.

WORKFLOW CHECKPOINTS THAT SCALE

Checkpoints are effective only when they are predictable and lightweight. In mature organizations, teams expect them and rely on them.

There are only three checkpoints that matter at scale:

- Entry (intake alignment)
- Shape (design and narrative alignment)

- Safety (pre-release validation)

Anything beyond these increases friction without reducing risk. Anything less allows drift to compound.

MANAGING HANDOFFS WITHOUT FRICTION

Handoffs are where search intent is most often lost. The role of process is to make expectations explicit at each transition.

SEO provides context, not instructions: evaluator intent, structural assumptions, and non-negotiable patterns. In return, SEO receives constraints—technical, legal, accessibility, or timing—that shape feasible solutions. When this exchange happens early, SEO stops being a late-stage blocker and becomes a stabilizing force.

DISTRIBUTED EXECUTION AND DRIFT CONTROL

As organizations scale, SEO cannot attend to every decision. The system must allow teams to make good choices independently.

This is achieved by clearly defining non-negotiables: template logic, narrative sequencing, and structural boundaries. Variation is permitted only where it does not alter interpretation. When teams understand where freedom exists and where it does not, local optimization no longer undermines global coherence.

COMPACT DECISION-RIGHTS MODEL (RACI)

The following table shows how responsibility is distributed across the SEO process lifecycle. It is intentionally compact to reflect how decisions actually occur at scale.

Process Domain	Visibility Ops	Product	Engineering	Content	Design
Intake alignment	A	R	C	C	C
Template & structural logic	A	C	R	C	C
Narrative flow & definitions	C	I	I	R	C
Implementation behavior	A	I	R	I	C
Pre-release validation	A	I	R	C	C
Post-release learning	A	C	C	C	I

Legend:
A = Accountable   R = Responsible   C = Consulted   I = Informed

This model does not centralize control. It ensures that accountability for system behavior is explicit, while execution remains distributed.

RAISING PROCESS MATURITY

Process maturity is visible when teams no longer need to be reminded of checkpoints, when intake quality improves without enforcement, and when regressions decline without heroics.

At that point, SEO is no longer a specialist intervention. It is part of how the organization builds things. Managerial effort shifts from correction to refinement, and visibility outcomes become more stable even as complexity increases.

WHY THIS PROCESS ENDURES

Processes fail when they rely on individual vigilance. They endure when they are embedded in normal work rhythms.

The framework in this chapter survives scale, turnover, and pressure because it minimizes steps, names responsibilities, and focuses only on decisions that materially affect visibility. It does not attempt to control creativity. It protects coherence.

That is the purpose of the process at an enterprise scale.

FURTHER READING

- **Book 2 — Accidental SEO Manager** — defines durable checkpoints, briefs, and decision moments that scale.
- **Book 4 — Is Our SEO Working?** — verifies whether process changes reduce regressions and improve clarity.

Chapter 28

SUSTAINING SEO AS A CONTINUOUS CAPABILITY

DEFINE THE CAPABILITY

Sustaining SEO over time depends on whether your organization treats it as a **durable capability with stable ownership**, funding, and an operating rhythm. Early wins can come from concentrated effort—fixing defects, cleaning up templates, publishing new content, addressing obvious technical constraints—but endurance comes from what happens after those wins stop feeling urgent. Visibility work must persist through reorgs, budget cycles, leadership turnover, platform changes, and shifting product priorities.

To define the capability, make the scope explicit in business terms. A continuous SEO capability covers three outcomes you can explain in an executive meeting without jargon:

- interpretability (systems can reliably understand what your pages mean),
- usability (evaluators can reliably progress through decisions), and
- operational stability (teams can change the site without creating drift).

When leaders can connect your work to those outcomes, sustaining support becomes more realistic because the capability has a purpose that survives individual initiatives.

A continuous capability also requires a "minimum viable operating model," even if it is lightweight. You want clarity on what stays funded, which decisions require review, and which routines happen regardless of the quarter's priorities. Without these anchors, SEO becomes personality-driven and episodic, and your ecosystem gradually returns to fragmentation.

Always-Funded Minimum

If you want the capability to endure, **define the minimum scope that stays funded even during cost pressure**. This baseline is maintenance and risk control. It is easier to protect a small, well-defined minimum than to defend an open-ended "SEO program" that looks discretionary.

Your always-funded minimum typically includes:

- **Template stewardship:** monitoring drift, maintaining pattern integrity, and preventing uncontrolled variation
- **Measurement integrity:** keeping instrumentation consistent enough to interpret movement reliably
- **Release risk review for structural changes:** ensuring high-impact changes have appropriate review depth
- **Content maintenance triage:** keeping top-value templates and pages accurate, current, and coherent
- **Incident readiness:** a clear response sequence when performance, indexing, or rendering shifts unexpectedly

When this minimum stays intact, you avoid the familiar cycle where a short funding dip creates drift that later requires an expensive recovery effort.

Defined Responsibilities

Endurance improves when responsibilities are documented in a way that other functions recognize. You want responsibility framed as decision rights and operational obligations, not as "SEO tasks." At minimum, you want clarity on:

- **Product:** prioritization, sequencing, and trade-off decisions that affect discoverability and clarity
- **Engineering:** implementation stability, rendering reliability, and change safety
- **Design:** component consistency, content presentation logic, and evaluator progression comfort
- **Content:** narrative accuracy, scenario flow, and definitional consistency
- **Legal and compliance:** constraints and disclosures that affect page structure and claims
- **Analytics:** measurement consistency, KPI governance, and instrumentation standards
- **Visibility Operations:** interpretation models, guardrails, portfolio risk management, and review depth rules

When these responsibilities are visible, SEO endures because it stops depending on a single function and "catching" problems early.

USE THE MATURITY MODEL TO MAKE ENDURANCE MEASURABLE

Chapter 6 referenced a five-level capability maturity model. Use it as a practical path to making SEO enduring, reframing sustainability as progression through observable capability levels rather than as ongoing persuasion. If leaders see a clear progression, they are more likely to fund the steps that move the organization forward.

Treat the model as a ladder from accidental outcomes to institutionalized control. The exact labels in your domain may vary, but the progression typically behaves like this:

Level 1 — Ad Hoc

Work depends on individuals, informal knowledge, and reactive fixes. Outcomes vary by team and quarter. Drift accumulates quietly because there is no systematic operating rhythm.

Your endurance move at this level is to define non-negotiables for templates and page purpose, then introduce a lightweight intake checkpoint for structural work.

Level 2 — Repeatable

Basic workflows exist and can be repeated. Teams know when to involve SEO, and there are recognizable checkpoints. The organization still relies on informal expertise, but execution becomes less chaotic.

Your endurance move at this level is to standardize a small set of patterns: template families, page types, and the minimum information required to begin work.

Level 3 — Defined

The capability has documented standards, clear ownership boundaries, and consistent terminology. Review depth is tied to change impact. Documentation starts carrying institutional memory.

Your endurance move at this level is to create a portfolio view: what templates exist, what is standard, what is exceptional, and where risk concentrates.

Level 4 — Managed

The organization manages the capability with operational metrics, predictable cadences, and clear escalation paths. Drift becomes detectable early, and corrective work is planned rather than improvised.

Your endurance move at this level is to run a stable rhythm of control: monthly portfolio health, quarterly lifecycle reviews, and a disciplined exception register with expiry dates.

Level 5 — Optimized

The capability improves continuously. Teams evolve templates and content deliberately without destabilizing meaning. Improvements compound because patterns are stable, instrumentation is consistent, and decision-making is disciplined.

Your endurance move at this level is to make controlled evolution routine: retire outdated templates, reduce exceptions, and institutionalize learning from incidents and releases into standards and components.

Progressing through these levels is itself an endurance strategy. It gives leaders a narrative that supports sustained investment: "We are moving from reactive reliability to managed stability to continuous optimization." It also gives you a diagnostic when enthusiasm dips: you can show which maturity behaviors are missing and what operational change would move you up one level.

RUN THE CADENCE

Enduring capabilities run on rhythm. Without rhythm, you get bursts of activity followed by decay. Your cadence should feel like operational hygiene rather than a special project. It must be light enough to survive busy quarters and structured enough to carry institutional memory.

A practical cadence has four layers: weekly triage, monthly governance, quarterly portfolio lifecycle work, and annual planning integration. You can adjust timing to your organization's pace, but the sequence matters because it keeps the system from drifting between major initiatives.

Weekly Triage

Weekly routines keep small issues from compounding. They also keep the organization's attention calibrated so you avoid emotional overreaction to noise.

A weekly triage cycle typically covers:

- Release risk scan for changes shipping this week that touch templates, navigation, routing, or metadata logic
- Drift sampling: a small, consistent sample of pages and templates to detect early divergence
- Exceptions review: new requests for variance, plus confirmation that old exceptions still have a valid reason
- Signal review: a short discussion of meaningful movement, emphasizing causes and actions rather than dashboards

The point is continuity. A stable weekly rhythm creates the conditions where SEO remains present without requiring constant escalation.

Monthly Operating Review

A monthly review is where you translate week-to-week activity into an executive-usable narrative. This is how you keep sponsorship alive without relying on crisis moments to earn attention.

A monthly review works best when it stays small:

- Portfolio health summary: stable, improving, or weakening across key template families
- Top risks: items that threaten interpretability, usability, or operational stability
- Decisions needed: two or three leadership choices, framed as trade-offs
- Evidence trail: what changed, what it caused, and what you will do next

When the review becomes predictable, leaders develop intuition for what "healthy" looks like. That familiarity is a major driver of endurance because it reduces fear when the ecosystem shifts.

Quarterly Portfolio Work

Quarterly routines prevent the slow decay that happens when a site grows without intentional maintenance. This is where you treat the site as a portfolio rather than as a single "website."

Your quarterly cycle should include:

- Template lifecycle review: which templates need refinement, which should be retired, which need consolidation
- Exception register cleanup: remove expired exceptions, renew those with a valid business case, convert frequent exceptions into standards
- Debt reduction allocation: a planned amount of capacity for eliminating structural inconsistency and instrumentation drift
- Training refresh: short reinforcement of patterns and decision logic for teams that ship structural changes

Quarterly work is where your capability becomes visible as an operational system, not a collection of best practices.

Annual Planning Integration

Endurance improves when SEO is integrated into annual planning rather than negotiated ad hoc. Your annual contribution is a capability plan: what you will stabilize, what you will improve, and what risks you will reduce.

Anchor the plan to the maturity model. Leaders will respond better to "we are moving from Defined to Managed" than to a long backlog. Use the maturity model as the narrative spine, then attach your year's priorities as the concrete steps that move the capability upward.

PROTECT THE PORTFOLIO

Enterprises manage portfolios: template families, component libraries, markets, products, platforms, and vendors. Sustaining SEO requires managing where risk concentrates and how variation is controlled. This is where many SEO programs fail: they discuss "consistency" as a principle without creating portfolio mechanisms that keep it real.

Your portfolio approach should make three things obvious:

- What is standard and stable
- What is exceptional and time-bound
- What is aging and approaching retirement

Template Families and Lifecycles

Treat templates as assets with lifecycles: design, adoption, saturation, refinement, and retirement. When templates remain in the ecosystem indefinitely, the organization inherits a shadow system where pages behave differently depending on when they were built. Evaluators experience inconsistency, and measurement becomes harder to interpret because performance changes have multiple structural causes.

A lifecycle practice keeps your ecosystem coherent:

- Name your template families and document their intended purpose
- Define permitted variants and the business reasons that justify them
- Establish retirement triggers, such as duplicated families, outdated assumptions, or recurring drift
- Plan migrations as staged choreography rather than as brute-force rewrites

When lifecycle discipline is in place, sustaining SEO becomes easier because you are maintaining a portfolio rather than fighting scattered fires.

Exception Registers with Expiry Dates

Exceptions rarely start as negligence. They start as "just for this release" decisions. Endurance requires controlling them. The simplest mechanism is an exception register with explicit expiry dates and owners. If an exception cannot survive being written down, it usually does not deserve to exist.

A workable register entry includes:

- What changed and where
- Why the exception exists
- Which standard does it diverge from
- The risk it introduces
- The owner who must either retire it or justify its renewal
- The expiry date or review date

This mechanism prevents drift from becoming permanent through inertia.

Portfolio Risk Concentration

Sustaining SEO requires an honest view of where risk concentrates. In many enterprises, a small number of template families, markets, and integrations drive most instability. You want to allocate protective attention to areas with a disproportionate impact.

Risk commonly concentrates in:

- High-volume templates that power many URLs
- Templates with heavy personalization or experimentation
- Region-specific variants with independent editing cultures
- Legacy stacks with inconsistent rendering paths

- Vendor-driven integrations that bypass component standards

A portfolio view helps you prioritize standardization where it matters and isolate variation where it is safer.

SURVIVE CHANGE WITHOUT LOSING THE MODEL

SEO endurance is tested during transitions: new leaders, reorganizations, acquisitions, migrations, and tooling shifts. During these moments, people solve local problems quickly, unintentionally weakening structural coherence. Your goal is to keep the operating model intact while allowing necessary change.

The 30-Minute Leader Brief

When a new executive sponsor arrives, you rarely get unlimited time. A brief can preserve your capability through leadership change if it focuses on what matters to them.

A practical brief covers:

- The capability definition: interpretability, usability, operational stability
- The maturity level today and the next level you are moving toward
- The cadence: what happens weekly and monthly to keep the system stable
- The portfolio view: where risk concentrates and why
- The two or three decisions you will need from leadership this quarter

This brief keeps the conversation anchored to a model rather than drifting into tactical debates.

Reorg and Turnover Handoffs

Turnover breaks fragile systems. Endurance depends on whether knowledge lives in structures rather than in a few people's memories. Your handoff package should be practical and minimal:

- Pattern library: page types and template families with purpose and non-negotiables
- Decision log: why key choices were made, with dates and owners
- Exception register: current variances and expiry dates
- Operating cadence: meeting rhythm and what each review produces
- Portfolio map: template families, markets, platforms, and vendor dependencies

When these artifacts exist, the capability survives because new contributors inherit clarity rather than improvisation.

EVOLVE WITHOUT DRIFT

Continuous capability requires change. The challenge is evolving deliberately without fragmenting the ecosystem. You need a model that classifies change by risk and ties it to review depth, validation, and post-release learning.

Classify Change by Impact

A simple classification improves endurance because it makes the right level of review feel normal:

- Routine: copy updates, small UX adjustments within existing components, minor internal linking refinements
- Structural: template layout changes, navigation updates, metadata logic changes, content model changes, instrumentation changes

243

- Critical: migrations, rendering framework changes, major template family changes, experimentation platform changes that can alter DOM structure at scale

Once change classes are defined, review depth stops feeling arbitrary. Teams know what happens next, and the system stays stable under delivery pressure.

Tie Review Depth to Shipping Gates

For structural and critical changes, define what must be true before shipping. Gates should evaluate behavior, not just checklists. High-value gates include:

- Template behavior validation across devices and key markets
- Confirmed component compliance and avoidance of unauthorized variants
- Instrumentation consistency checks for key events and properties
- Confirmed narrative integrity: page purpose, definitional consistency, scenario flow

Shipping gates preserve stability by preventing the most common endurance failure: local speed creating global drift.

Convert Learning into Standards

Endurance improves when learning becomes institutional memory rather than tribal knowledge. When an incident or release reveals a weakness, treat the outcome as a pattern update:

- Update the pattern library so future teams inherit the fix
- Adjust components so the correct behavior becomes the default
- Update the decision log with rationale so people understand why the standard exists

This is how continuous improvement becomes real: the system gradually carries more of the burden, and teams rely less on heroics.

MAKE THE CAPABILITY FELT ACROSS ROLES

A continuous capability becomes durable when every function experiences it as helpful rather than as overhead. That requires translating SEO into the outcomes each function already values: fewer regressions, faster launches, clearer decisions, and fewer escalations.

Product supports endurance when SEO reduces roadmap friction and avoids late rework. Engineering supports endurance by reducing ambiguous requirements and making releases safer. Design supports endurance when components remain coherent, and evaluator progression stays smooth. Content supports endurance when narrative patterns reduce revision cycles and improve comprehension. Analytics supports endurance when instrumentation is consistent enough to interpret movement with confidence.

The maturity model helps here as well. Each function can see what "better" looks like at the next level, and you can align training and routines to the behaviors that move the organization upward.

FURTHER READING

- **Book 2 — Accidental SEO Manager** — embeds habits, rituals, and ownership that make SEO endure.
- **Book 4 — Is Our SEO Working?** — supports learning loops and longitudinal evaluation of stability.

Chapter 29

CRISIS MANAGEMENT AND RECOVERY PROTOCOLS

USING THIS CHAPTER IN A CRISIS

This chapter is designed for use under time pressure. Start with the Crisis Index to identify the type of incident you are facing. Then follow the First-Hour Protocol and the relevant playbook. Do not read this chapter sequentially during an incident. Jump to the section that matches the symptoms you see.

The goal of crisis management is containment, preservation of meaning, and disciplined recovery. Speed comes from clarity, not from certainty.

CRISIS INDEX (START HERE)

Use the symptom that best matches what you are observing. This is not an exhaustive list.

- Traffic or impressions dropped sharply across many pages overnight
  → Performance Shock
- Pages disappeared from search, large sections no longer visible
  → Indexing and Discovery Failure
- Templates rendering incorrectly, missing sections, broken navigation
  → Structural Template Failure

- Site is slow, content not loading, interactions broken
  → Technical Instability
- Spam pages, injected links, hacked titles, or redirects
  → Security Breach
- Migration or replatform launch caused widespread volatility
  → Migration Failure
- Consent banner, A/B testing tool, widget, broke layout or content
  → Third-Party Dependency Failure
- Brand controversy or negative press driving sudden demand
  → Reputational Flashpoint
- Analytics stopped reporting, or the data is clearly wrong
  → Measurement Outage

FIRST-HOUR PROTOCOL (ALL CRISES)

This protocol applies to every crisis type.

Contain

- Freeze risky deployments and scheduled publishes
- Isolate affected templates, sections, or markets
- Capture before/after examples (URLs, screenshots, behaviors)

Classify

- Name the crisis type using the index
- Estimate scope (which templates, markets, journeys)
- Decide rollback vs isolation bias

Command

- Incident lead (overall coordination)
- Technical lead (engineering/platform)
- Content or communications lead

- Analytics lead

Set update cadence (30–60 minutes initially). Use one shared log. Undocumented actions do not occur.

Communicate

Use a fixed update format:

- Situation
- Scope
- Actions taken
- Blockers
- Next checkpoint

Avoid speculation. Clarity stabilizes teams faster than optimism.

STRUCTURAL TEMPLATE FAILURE PLAYBOOK

Symptoms

- Missing sections, reordered explanations
- Broken internal linking
- Template behaving differently across markets or devices

Confirm / Rule Out

- Did a component, CMS change, or config deploy recently?
- Is behavior consistent across environments?

Contain

- Freeze affected templates

Recovery

- Restore intended explanatory order
- Reinstate expected linking patterns
- Verify meaning, not just layout

Executive Update

- What broke (behavior)
- What was restored
- What remains frozen

TECHNICAL INSTABILITY PLAYBOOK

Symptoms

- Pages are slow or failing to load
- Content missing due to JS or rendering issues
- Navigation or interactions broken

Contain

- Shift to safe-mode behavior
- Disable fragile scripts or personalization
- Prioritize loading of critical content

Recovery

- Restore evaluator-visible behavior first
- Verify on representative devices
- Short verification loops (every five minutes)

Trap to Avoid

- Chasing diagnostics instead of user experience

SECURITY BREACH PLAYBOOK

Symptoms

- Spam pages indexed
- Injected links, titles, or redirects
- Unauthorized content appearing

Contain

- List compromised URLs or patterns
- Remove, noindex, or block contaminated surfaces
- Coordinate with security on access lockdown

Recovery

- Restore clean templates from backup
- Validate that contaminated patterns are gone

Communication

- Minimal, factual external statements
- One canonical explanation is that evaluators were exposed

PERFORMANCE SHOCK PLAYBOOK

Symptoms

- Sudden ranking or impression collapse
- Volatility across stable templates

Parallel Lanes

- Internal change review (what shipped)
- External landscape scan (what shifted)
- Structural health check (what decayed)

Contain

- Roll back internal regressions if identified
- Do not rewrite broadly

Recovery

- Restore clarity on core pages
- Reinforce purpose, flow, and connections
- Let performance recover from stability

INDEXING AND DISCOVERY FAILURE PLAYBOOK

Symptoms

- Important pages missing from results
- Sections partially or inconsistently visible

Contain

- Restore straightforward access to core information
- Reverse changes that hid meaning or navigation

Recovery

- Clarify page purpose
- Reinforce internal connections
- Validate discovery in affected sections only

MIGRATION FAILURE PLAYBOOK

Symptoms

- Widespread volatility after launch
- Meaning or navigation altered at scale

Contain

- Revert the riskiest change first
- Reinstate previous explanatory order

Recovery

- Validate behavior on a controlled slice
- Expand gradually once stability holds

Trap to Avoid

- Fixing only what tools flag instead of what evaluators experience

THIRD-PARTY DEPENDENCY FAILURE PLAYBOOK

Symptoms

- Layout shifts, missing content, blocked interactions
- Failures tied to scripts or widgets

Contain

- Disable or sandbox the dependency
- Restore core experience first

Recovery

- Decide whether to isolate, harden, or retire the integration
- Record ownership and review cadence

REPUTATIONAL FLASHPOINT PLAYBOOK

Symptoms

- Sudden demand for explanations about the organization
- Misinformation fills gaps

Contain

- Create one canonical explainer
- Coordinate phrasing across channels

Recovery

- Add timestamped updates and Q&A
- De-escalate carefully after the event

Trap to Avoid

- Multiple uncoordinated pages competing for authority

MEASUREMENT OUTAGE PLAYBOOK

Symptoms

- Analytics unavailable or clearly wrong
- Loss of the decision signal during another incident

Contain

- Stand up minimal backup signals
- Focus on direction, not precision

Recovery

- Restore instrumentation
- Schedule data-quality review post-incident

RECOVERY AND RESTORATION

Restore Patterns

- Reconnect internal linking
- Verify template integrity
- Remove emergency inconsistencies

Restore Narrative

- Clean rushed edits
- Re-establish clear purpose and flow

Recovery is not complete until meaning, connections, and predictability are restored.

AFTER-ACTION LEARNING

Within one week, capture:

- Trigger
- Missed signals
- Decisions that helped
- Friction points
- One pattern or guardrail to update

Assign owners and dates. Share a one-page summary. Crises become capability only when learning is institutionalized.

PRACTICING READINESS

Run quarterly tabletop exercises. Rotate scenarios. Practice the first hour. Each exercise must produce one permanent improvement to playbooks, dashboards, or release gates.

A calm, practiced response is a capability. Panic is optional.

RETURNING TO NORMAL

Resume normal cadence deliberately. Avoid permanent over-controls. Restore confidence by showing stability, not by memorializing the incident.

A crisis handled well strengthens trust. One handled poorly leaves scars that last longer than the outage itself.

FURTHER READING

- **Book 2—Accidental SEO Manager**—strengthens crisis orchestration, communication, and cross-team focus.
- **Book 4—Is Our SEO Working?**—helps diagnose shocks, track recovery, and document lessons.

Chapter 30

STAYING CURRENT AND PREPARING FOR THE FUTURE

THE REAL NATURE OF CHANGE

Search does not change in isolated bursts; it evolves continuously through interface shifts, new interpretive layers, and changing evaluator behavior. What feels disruptive is rarely the pace of change itself, but the lack of internal readiness to absorb it calmly. Organizations struggle not because they missed a feature announcement, but because their systems cannot adapt without destabilizing clarity, governance, or decision-making.

You must ensure that your organization can absorb change without panic, regression, or fragmentation. That capability—adaptation without drift—is the defining skill of modern SEO leadership.

FILTERING MATTERS MORE THAN FORECASTING

The volume of industry commentary has grown faster than its signal. New tools, theories, and predictions appear weekly, many framed as urgent or existential. Reacting to all of them weakens credibility and exhausts teams. Strategic leadership requires disciplined filtering.

You evaluate change through first principles: does it alter how evaluators understand information, how meaning is assembled, or how trust is formed? If it does not, it is noise. This filtering protects the organization from reaction cycles and preserves focus on structural improvements that compound over time.

PREPARING FOR AI INTERPRETATION WITHOUT CHASING IT

AI-driven surfaces do not eliminate the need for websites; they increase the importance of clarity, structure, and internal coherence. Systems that summarize, extract, or recombine information depend on the same fundamentals that humans do: clear purpose, stable narrative flow, and explicit relationships between concepts.

Preparing for AI interpretation is a continuation of disciplined content design, predictable templates, and intentional linking. When meaning is explicit, it survives extraction. When it is ambiguous, no optimization rescues it. The future favors organizations that invest in interpretability rather than novelty.

DESIGNING FOR PARTIAL VISIBILITY

Increasingly, evaluators encounter fragments rather than full pages—summaries, highlights, answers, or excerpts. This reality changes how risk accumulates. If critical meaning appears late, depends on context, or requires visual cues to interpret, it degrades under partial exposure.

Future-ready organizations design so essential meaning survives truncation. Purpose statements, definitions, and core explanations appear early and consistently. This discipline benefits every surface equally: traditional search, AI summaries, voice responses, and emerging interfaces.

CAPABILITY OUTLASTS TACTICS

Tools and techniques age quickly. Capabilities endure. The organizations that remain effective are not those that mastered every update, but those that built shared reasoning across product, design, engineering, content, and analytics.

That capability is reflected in how decisions are made: whether teams understand evaluator intent, whether structural changes are assessed for risk, whether governance guides rather than blocks, and whether learning compounds release by release. These behaviors matter more than any single optimization.

PROGRESSION MATTERS MORE THAN MATURITY

This book introduces a five-level capability maturity model to describe how organizations evolve in their handling of visibility. Preparing for the future does not require reaching the highest level. Few organizations ever do, and that is not the objective.

What matters is **directional progress**. A Level 2 organization that is deliberately strengthening intake, documentation, and cross-functional clarity is more future-ready than a stagnant Level 4 organization drifting under its own complexity. Movement through the levels—however gradual—is itself a form of resilience.

Staying current means helping the organization move forward from where it is now, not holding it to an idealized end state.

GOVERNANCE THAT EVOLVES WITHOUT BREAKING

As new surfaces and behaviors emerge, governance must adapt without becoming brittle. Rules tied too tightly to formats decay quickly. Principles tied to meaning, clarity, and responsibility endure.

Future-proof governance clarifies who owns decisions, which patterns must remain stable, and where controlled variation is acceptable. It evolves through small, deliberate adjustments rather than periodic overhauls. When governance remains principle-driven, teams adapt confidently instead of improvising under pressure.

BUILDING ORGANIZATIONAL JUDGMENT

The most valuable skill you develop is judgment: the ability to interpret change, weigh risk, and guide decisions without overreacting. Judgment grows through reflection, not speed. It strengthens when you review outcomes honestly, document reasoning, and teach others how to think—not what to copy.

Organizations with strong judgment do not chase the future. They meet it calmly, because their internal logic is sound.

PREPARING THE ORGANIZATION, NOT JUST YOURSELF

A capability that depends on one individual is fragile. Preparing for the future means transferring reasoning into the organization—through playbooks, shared language, predictable workflows, and repeated reinforcement.

When new contributors join, they should inherit clarity rather than ambiguity. When leadership changes, the system should remain intelligible. When pressure increases, teams should fall back on stable habits rather than improvisation. That continuity is the true measure of readiness.

A PRACTICAL OPERATING CADENCE FOR VISIBILITY

Staying current does not require constant reaction or perfect foresight. It requires a steady operating cadence that allows you to detect change early, interpret it calmly, and adjust without destabilizing the system. The most resilient organizations do not chase every shift in search or in AI behavior; they rely on simple, repeatable rhythms that maintain clarity, structure, and accountability over time.

This cadence is not a checklist and not a maturity target. It does not assume Level 5 capability or advanced tooling. Progress at any level comes from consistently applying the same disciplines, even when resources are constrained. What matters is movement from reactive handling toward predictable stewardship.

The following rhythm summarizes the managerial posture described throughout this book.

Always
Guard clarity, structure, and stability as content, templates, and definitions evolve.

Weekly
Scan for anomalies and early signals before they escalate into structural problems.

Monthly
Review coverage, performance, intent alignment, and structural consistency on priority surfaces.

Quarterly
Assess portfolio-level risk, governance effectiveness, and alignment with business objectives.

On Change
Review before and after every significant release, migration, or definition shift.

Annually
Reassess maturity, ownership, and long-term visibility risk—not to optimize, but to simplify.

ENDING WHERE IT BEGAN

The future of search will continue to evolve, but its direction is consistent: faster comprehension, clearer meaning, and reduced tolerance for ambiguity. Organizations that invest in clarity, coherence, and disciplined decision-making remain effective regardless of surface changes.

You do not prepare for the future by chasing it. You prepare by building systems that endure—systems that progress steadily through maturity, absorb change without panic, and preserve meaning under pressure. That is how SEO becomes not just current, but sustainable.

FURTHER READING

- **Book 2—Accidental SEO Manager**—builds adaptable leadership, influence, and calm decision-making under change.
- **Book 4 — Is Our SEO Working?** — shows how to measure readiness, interpret shifts, and validate new patterns

INDEX

www.ingramcontent.com/pod-product-compliance
Lightning Source LLC
Chambersburg PA
CBHW080906170526
45158CB00008B/2010